ADVANCE

On the Presidential Campaign Trail

STEVEN JACQUES

Acheson Editions

Washington, D.C.

Advance/Acheson Editions
Printed in the United States of America

Although every precaution has been taken to verify the accuracy of the information contained herein, the author and publisher assume no responsibility for any errors or omissions. No liability is assumed for damages that may result from the use of information contained within.

Advance/ Steven Jacques -- 1st ed.

ISBN 9798300688011 Print Edition

CONTENTS

ACKNOWLEDGEMENTS

It is with deep gratitude that I acknowledge the following incredibly kind people who have helped me in this peculiar career and in my life:

First and always - my long suffering and consistently loving parents, Frances and Clemens, who not so much "helped" as "enabled" everything from start to finish. No finer people ever lived. No better role models ever raised a family.

Speaking of role models to whom I owe my thanks: Judge Richard Franks, Bob Gaines, Jim and Nora Denbo, Vlad and Nancy Sambaiew, Kim Scott, Gus West, Linda Crew, Aram and Kathryn Kailian, Congressman Emanuel Cleaver, Phil Scaglia, Bill Lacy, Kelly Cox, Antonia Felix, Tom Trapasso, Steve Diminuco, Gary Barber, Dan O'Connell, and the entire Carter-Mondale, Clinton-Gore, Kerry-Edwards, Obama-Biden and Harris-Walz advance community, who are my sisters and brothers.

In memoriam: Jim King, the yoda of Democratic political operatives, Bobby McDevitt, who attacked life as a happy warrior, and Congressman Jerry Litton, who would have been president one day.

And a heartfelt thank you to my beautiful and talented wife, Christine Colby Jacques, a Broadway baby and true legend, who is my rock and my inspiration. In addition to everything else, not surprisingly she also made this book better.

ADVANCE

CHAPTER 1

Getting Started, 1976 Carter-Mondale
Campaign, Disaster in Santa Ana

To paraphrase the poet Edward Thomas, much is written about politics, far less about the journey. For those who are national political operatives known as "advance," it is all about the journey.

There is no other job in the entire world like presidential-level advance. It is the most stressful and most romanticized role in national politics. No other job allows you to travel the entire country, sometimes the world, and forces you to become an intimate, if brief, part of dozens of communities' civic lives. You connect with a universe of people in a way experienced by no traveling salesman, no journalists, no politicians, no anthropologists and no beauty contest winners at any level. It's also the most fun and the most challenging thing you can do in politics, especially if you are fresh out college, or still in college as I was when I started.

No other job asks you to produce a 30,000-person rally in three days, in a town you've never visited before, with the national media and a presidential candidate breathing down your neck as you witness success or failure together in real time. If you screw it up, all they have to do is never send you out on another advance. Sudden death without a phone call.

Imagine doing that every four or five days for months on end.

The young men and women, (and eventually not-so-young), who do presidential advance, descend on a town, immediately meet and work with key civic leaders and a big slice of the community (both activists and plain old every day folks who have no idea what's about to hit them), wander anywhere and go behind the scenes wherever, then create an entire eco-system in a few days, if they're lucky, sometimes only one or two days if they're not, often involving thousands of people, surrounding a visit that is guaranteed to be historic on some level because it will be covered by the national news media.

Advance is the ultimate All-Access Pass and the Ultimate Political Challenge.

It's akin to bringing the circus to town, but with a mission. Instead of profits, the seamlessness of the events and, ultimately, winning the day's news coverage determine success or failure.

Any time national media attention is focused on an event there will be pressure, but there also are subtle concerns that are equally important. Behind the scenes are usually dozens or hundreds of people who will always remember the experience of working with the advance team. Good advance staffers keep that in mind. No one who participates in the preparations for a presidential, or presidential candidate's, visit will ever forget the experience.

Generally, everyone who merely attends a major presidential campaign event or presidential visit remembers it for the rest of his or her life too.

As a result, advance staff cannot create ill-will. It's called leaving blood.

The best advance "agents," as Theodore H. White described them in his historic book, *The Making of the President, 1960,* "are practitioners of one of the most complicated skills in American politics." A good advance person "must combine . . . the qualities of a circus tout, a carnival organizer, an accomplished diplomat and a quartermaster general."

The art and craft of presidential campaign advance, the way we understand it in the modern era, was invented by the Kennedy campaign in 1959 and '60. They started sending small teams of political operatives, all advance "men" in those days, to control all aspects of John Kennedy's appearances. Teams were usually one to three young men.

They were completely responsible for the local arrangements—the politics, the production of rallies and political events of all kinds, the press, the crowds, the labor unions, volunteers, motorcades—for the primary purpose of controlling that 30-to-45 seconds of national TV news coverage they hoped to get on NBC, CBS and ABC.

Then there's this additional fun fact: In those days, the advance team also had to raise the money to pay for everything . . . all the production, rentals, hotels, anything that cost money. They either had to raise the money to pay for it, get it donated, "borrow" it, or talk people into sending the bill to headquarters. The latter two often didn't work out well for the donors/vendors.

By 1976, the 1960s was referred to as "the days of buccaneer advance." Advance teams were infamous for leaving blood when they left town because they had a reputation for leaving unpaid bills, "borrowing" cars for motorcades, stepping on local officials' toes, or myriad other offenses. It was slash and burn advance. When Kennedy's private plane "Caroline" lifted-off, the advance guys would call national headquarters to report "wheels-up" from the closest pay phone at the airport, then take the next flight out of there.

As an aside, even as late as 1980, advance trainees were instructed to keep a roll of quarters in their pockets to make phone calls.

The most renowned of presidential advance men from that early era was Jim King, who started working for John Kennedy in the late 50s and eventually worked in senior roles for Bobby, Ted, John Kerry, President Carter, and President Clinton. He also ran the podium for the Democratic National Convention for twenty-four years and the entire Massachusetts Democratic Convention for forty years. He was a respected and exceptionally popular institution in national Democratic politics.

Friendly and large at six-foot-three and over two hundred and twenty pounds, Jim was an imposing figure. He had a Boston accent that might have found a home on the docks, coupled with a keen eye for observation, a brilliant analytic mind, and charisma. Lots of charisma. He was as engaging one-on-one as he was in front of an audience and seemingly never uttered a word that wasn't insightful. Always just slightly rumpled, he was perpetually attired in a nondescript sport coat, khakis, and running shoes, although they were apparently never used as such.

Back in the 60s, in the days when it was acceptable to do anything, say anything or promise anything to ensure that the events were successful, Jim never left a drop of blood needlessly. His charm and charisma would have allowed him to get away with a lot, but he was always aware that people would judge the candidate by the actions of the advance team. His simple decency played a hand too.

There was a story that went around that he once elbowed an elderly lady in the ribs because she wouldn't let go of Bobby Kennedy's arm while the convertible that Bobby was riding in was pulling away. It may have been apocryphal.

My own odyssey through forty some-odd years in national politics began when Jim King hired me to serve in Jimmy Carter's presidential campaign in 1976 as a member of the national staff doing Advance for then-Governor Carter.

Carter's presidential campaign called upon Jim in the summer of 1976 to help them prepare for Fall. Among other tasks, he created, designed and ran the best advance training school ever to bless a presidential campaign. In my opinion, it has never been equaled in either concept, production or educational impact.

Invitees to the two-day advance training session at the Peachtree Plaza Hotel in Atlanta were being evaluated from the moment they arrived at the airport and connected with their drivers. The "drivers" were staff members from the campaign's office of scheduling and advance who transported groups of attendees to the hotel, and those staff members kept notes. If one of the invitees was asked to help with luggage or some other small tasks, their attitude and demeanor were noted. None of the invitees were aware of it, of course.

Everyone arrived on a Friday afternoon, and the first event was an evening reception with an open bar, for which there was a practical reason. As Jim King recounted years later, everyone was watched and anyone who had too many drinks was sent home the next day. It happened to a couple of people.

The next morning's training began promptly at 8 a.m. in the ballroom, at which time the doors to the ballroom were closed and locked. Anyone who arrived after 8:00:01 was sent home. It happened to a few people.

Seminars on site preparation, crowd building, press relations, interaction with Secret Service and logistics were all punctuated with Jim King's wisdom and wit.

He was a strong proponent of the Lead advance's role in controlling everything, both during the advance and throughout the event or events. Once the candidate arrived, it was the Lead's responsibility to physically lead him through both the logistical and political elements of the trip.

Jim was also adamant about one thing: An advance person never "clutches." It was the cardinal sin of the Carter campaign. If it even LOOKED like you were more interested in hanging out with the candidate, or whatever celebrity might be involved with a given event, than you were in doing your job, the campaign would send you home. Surprisingly, given human nature, it was rare.

Jim's quote during the training seminar was, "If you have to brief Governor Carter, try do it in the holding room. If you have to do it in public, do it and get out of the way. If we see your picture on television or in a major national publication standing within ten feet of the candidate, we will guarantee you a bus ticket to within fifty miles of your home."

Another of Jim's quotes, stressing the importance of ensuring the press's access to events, was, "I don't care if a million people attended your event; if the press didn't get there to cover it, it never happened."

He had a way of making his points in graphic and memorable ways.

Jim chose and trained his national advance staff well, but there were still mishaps. During the Carter campaign in '76, when something went horribly wrong during an event, it was referred to as an "abortion." There were probably eight or nine notable abortions during the 1976 general election.

Among the most notable was the Mexican Independence Day Parade in September in Santa Ana, California, in which Jimmy Carter was scheduled to walk with Governor Jerry Brown. At the end of the parade there was a stage, sort of a bandstand-looking contraption, where Gov. Carter would give a speech.

In an era when three-person advance teams were the norm, Carter's weekend of activities in Southern California required eighteen, of whom I was most junior. I was slated to help with sites.

Carter was to appear in several locations, including the parade, and afterward a barbecue at the ranch of a wealthy Democratic donor. That event included Hollywood celebrities.

Also in tow—more than eighty members of the traveling press. They were journalists from all of the major newspapers, magazines, and radio and national television networks, including their camera crews with hundreds of pounds of bulky equipment, as well as local press who opted to travel on the press plane, the "zoo plane," for that portion of Carter's trip.

The question was how to transport them during the parade. They were there to cover Carter, and Carter wanted the coverage, but they couldn't be expected to walk along for the entire mile and a half, even with advance staffers keeping them corralled with a walking rope line. It would have been chaos.

A solution was devised by members of the advance team who were responsible for press. These wise old media pros—probably almost thirty years of age—decided the solution was to transport the press in two cattle trucks with open beds and tall wood slats for sides. If a cattle truck could safely transport cows, why not press? The press could stand and watch over the sides to keep an eye on Carter, camera crews could take video from that perch.

From the advance team's perspective, the press would be able to ride, not forced to walk, *and* be contained. At the end of the parade, the trucks would perform a second duty as press platforms to watch/cover Carter's speech. The trucks' bed heights were almost as tall as the stage.

The trucks could pull-up directly in front of the stage. Brilliant. A traveling press area with built-in riser.

The advance team Lead for the entire weekend in Southern California, a veteran political operative in his mid-thirties, had advanced the parade route and stage area and determined it would work.

No one thought to sweep out and sanitize the truck beds from the previous inhabitants' travels. *(I mean, come on, the press won't mind, will they?)*

Carter and Brown arrived on schedule separately at the parade. The Carter press' busses emptied their riders into the cattle trucks as planned.

As the two governors began their walk along the mile-and-a-half-long parade route, one unhappy fact became apparent. There was no one watching the parade along the route. No one. It was deadly. About every hundred feet they passed a tiny cluster of people on one or the other side of the road.

After a half mile Carter was visibly not pleased. Driving in front of Carter and Brown, in the two cattle trucks, those eighty some-odd cynical, sarcastic, tired, handled, and now smelly, members of the press were becoming amused.

One journalist, a novelist and TV gossip columnist named Barbara Howar, began to moo. Soon, eighty some-odd members of the traveling press corps were mooing like cows.

Sam Donaldson, covering Carter for ABC, kept jumping off his truck and running ahead when he saw a pay telephone; he'd make a quick call to somebody, then run and catch up with his cattle truck again. He did it a few times, only he knew why.

Jim King, in his role as trip director, was right there. He carried a portable loudspeaker slung over his shoulder so he could direct people when necessary, and as he watched the scene unfold, he began a color commentary for the benefit of the press and the few people watching from the sidelines.

"Ladies and gentlemen," he announced in his Boston accent, "the people mooing like cows are distinguished members of the national press corps. Our guests this afternoon include Miss Barbara Howar, Mr. Sam Donaldson . . . " and he continued for several more.

Jim opined, "You will notice they are caged like wild beasts, as they should be, for your protection. Please keep your hands away from their enclosures as they have not been fed yet."

Several minutes of running commentary followed as the parade lumbered along at a walking pace, witnessed by tens of people, and after a while the press tired of mooing.

Carter, when he wasn't happy with the way things were going at an event, would look for his advance staff. He would look for them and then look at them. It was unsettling for the poor unfortunates who suffered this fate either through their own incompetence or circumstances beyond their control. The Mexican Independence Day Parade was both.

The Lead advance should have known that a mile-and-a-half walk was too long, and that the crowd along the route would be sparse because everyone would gather at the end of the parade route where all the festivities and food booths were. This happened to be in front of the stage where Carter would speak.

The parade was deadly. Carter glared at his Lead. Advance staffers who were lower on food chain hid from Carter's view.

It only got worse at the end.

The two trucks pulled up in front of the stage, as directed. However, the advance team had neglected to gauge the impact two large trucks would have on the five thousand people standing on the other side of those trucks. All in a moment, most of the crowd could no longer see the stage. They weren't happy and they were vocal about it.

Santa Ana's mayor took the microphone and tried to energize the crowd. He gave a rousing introduction for Carter, ending with "Let's give a lusty welcome to Governor Jimmy Carter."

It hadn't been two weeks since Carter's unusual "lust in my heart" interview that appeared in Playboy Magazine, which caused a media sensation the Carter campaign preferred to have forgotten. Maybe the mayor thought he was being funny. It wasn't funny to Carter or his traveling or advance staffs, but it was pretty funny to the confined members of the traveling press.

(Incidentally, it may sound like it's better to amuse the national press corps than to piss them off, but it's worse. Given their circumstances, where they are captives on airplanes and in motorcades and hotels for days on end, they are usually irritated about something. Adding "amusement" gives them fodder to vent their pique.)

After he finished his speech, Governor Carter looked around for his advance team members. Junior members of the team were fortunate to have duties far away. Senior members, the Lead and Press 1, weren't so fortunate.

There was no time for immediate recriminations after Carter wrapped-up his speech. The advance Lead remained at a distance, and Press 1 stayed with the press, and Governor Brown remained with Carter as they were whisked away via motorcade to Rancho Mission Viejo for the DNC barbecue.

Brown brought his date, a tall redhead, along in the limo with Carter. Brown's driver, a California State Patrolman, followed in the governor's car behind the motorcade.

Three air-conditioned trailers were on-site at the barbecue—one for the advance team to use as an office, one for Carter to use as his "hold," and one for the Secret Service. All had telephones installed.

Among the celebrities enjoying the festivities was one member of a popular folk-rock band who arrived in his Rolls Royce convertible after Carter and Brown had arrived. He rolled slowly out of the driver's side door wearing a brown t-shirt that appeared to be wet on the front. When he meandered to the bar and downed a couple shots of tequila, it became apparent where the moisture came from. It was the angels' portion—the amount of tequila that didn't make it all the way to his mouth and would, instead, flow down and eventually evaporate into the heavens. A lovely way of looking at it, at least.

After he meandered to the bar he meandered toward Carter and Brown, who had a lovely time alternately listening and then responding to his keen observations about the world situation for several minutes. Carter was remarkably kind. He didn't seem pleased but he was kind.

Brown must have been used to that kind of behavior from his years in public life in La-La Land.

One aside: On a positive note, that rock star is still alive and kicking as of this writing in 2024.

Another aside: Two days prior to event day, I was in the office of Mr. O'Neill, the owner of the gazillion-acre spread known as Rancho Mission Viejo. I was tasked with finalizing arrangements for delivery of two trailers (one for Carter's holding room and the other as an Advance office) the Advance team needed on-site.

In the middle of his meeting, O'Neill's secretary came in and announced that Warren Beatty was on the phone and wanted to talk to Governor Carter's Advance man.

I was handed the phone and introduced myself.

"Nice to meet you" was Mr. Beatty's response. "Say, I'd like to get the phone number for Governor Carter's trailer at the barbecue."

As a naïve, easily intimidated political operative in my first presidential campaign, my first thought was, "How the hell did Warren Beatty know there was a telephone in the trailer?"

My second thought was an agonized, "What the hell do I do? The guy is one of the hosts." I had the phone numbers in my notebook but was under the impression they should be kept confidential. On the other hand, I didn't want to piss-off someone who could squash me like a bug.

I finally politely offered, "Mr. Beatty, I'm going to have to get that from my Lead. Could you give me your phone number and let me get back to you?"

The phone went dead. My third thought was, "Oh shit, I'm gonna hear about that."

Later in the day, when I reported to my Lead about the incident, I heard what I wanted to hear. The Lead growled, "If you had given Beatty that phone number, I would have sent you home."

It was easy to get sent home.

The barbecue, other than the drunken rock star incident, went well. After about an hour, Carter and his retinue of staff, Secret Service, and press corps departed in the motorcade, followed by Governor Brown's car driven by his state patrolman.

The site advance team, as always, remained on-site to finish their tasks and depart separately. We were in the staff trailer when we heard a loud knock on the side. Looking out, we saw Governor Brown, with the tall redhead standing next to him.

Brown was fuming; he was stranded. His driver assumed that Brown and his date were still with Carter and had gotten into Carter's limo as before. As a result, the governor's driver and car were following the motorcade.

The Site 1 advance guy looked around to the team. "Who's got a car we could give to the governor?" One of them pulled out a set of car keys and handed them to the Site guy.

"Here governor, take one of ours. It's the white van over there." He pointed to a grimy twelve-passenger Ford that looked a little worse for wear. Brown said a terse "thank you" and took the keys. He and his friend drove off in the van. The advance team never found out what happened to it, but we assumed it was returned to the rental agency.

Election Night, November 2, 1976

Election night festivities were held in the World Congress Center at the Omni in Atlanta. Along with individual hotel rooms for each national advance staff member, they had a private suite for the entire Advance staff to congregate. Many of the team were actively participating in the operations of election night events, so the Advance Staff suite was hopping all evening and many lounged on the chairs and couches to watch TV coverage.

At one point, just before 8 p.m., Governor Carter's brother Billy arrived at the hotel near a gaggle of reporters, some of whom were reporting live. Several put microphones in his face and asked him how he was feeling about the evening.

Well, Billy was feeling very good about the evening. He appeared to be feeling a little too good for the Advance people watching the coverage on television. It was a national television news feed.

They assumed he had been drinking too much and they began to laugh as he fumbled through the questions. In one instant, the suite fell silent. They all realized the same fact at the same moment, like a mystical political epiphany. One of them said it: "The polls are still open on the West Coast." A dozen Advance staffers sprang from their comfy seats and headed to the stairwell, not the elevator, and ran down to the front of the hotel, where the first one to reach the scene smiled nicely and stepped in front of the cameras while the other Advance people greeted Billy warmly as they congregated around him, then walked with him into the hotel. They remained with him as he was escorted up the elevator to the Carters' family suite, which didn't have liquor in it.

At 10 p.m. that night, as the outcome remained in doubt, the director of Advance handed out Carter/Mondale National Advance Staff t-shirts to commemorate the general election. On the back was printed a list of events that went wrong—the so-called "abortions." Near the top of the list was the Mexican Independence Day Parade in Santa Ana.

The election wasn't called until almost 4 a.m. Shortly thereafter, Jimmy Carter appeared in the World Congress Center to give his acceptance speech surrounded by family, close friends, and over twenty thousand supporters who remained to witness the historic moment. His comments were brief due to the late hour, but the crowd's enthusiasm was not dimmed. There was a sense of moral destiny among those who had worked to get him elected.

The next day, campaign manager Hamilton Jordan, along with a few other senior campaign officials, stood before the entire Carter campaign staff in a large hotel meeting room to tell everyone what was to happen going forward. Every soul in the room wanted to know how he or she could play a role in the new administration.

Hamilton was optimistic and appreciative as he explained as much of the process as he could, and his ultimate message was simple enough. "All of you will get jobs in the new administration. Go home and you'll be hearing from us."

It was easy to get sent home. Some heard, most didn't.

Thankfully, I wasn't looking for a job. I thought I was too young for a full-time position. My plan was to return to college, where I'd dropped out in the fourth semester of my sophomore year to take the campaign job for Carter. As a student, I was available to do official Advance trips for the White House when they called, and I was willing to take the salary they offered, which was no salary at all . . . only per diem and the honor of doing Advance around the country and the world for the President or the Vice President of the United States. Plenty of people were willing to work for per diem, including me.

Almost two years later, in the Spring of 1978, my friend Bob Gaines, a colleague from the 1976 campaign and long-time big-time Chicago political operator, was asked to lead an Advance for Vice President Mondale to Carbondale, Illinois. Gaines asked the White House to assign me as his "second" on a two-person team.

The vice president was scheduled to speak at an event for Sen. Paul Simon. Sen. Simon's friend, actor Eddie Albert of Green Acres TV show fame, was the master of ceremonies, and Mr. Albert was as handsome in person as he was on television.

Serendipitously, the vice president's Director of Advance, Bill Roberts, was traveling with the vice president, serving as Trip Director, the day of our events in Carbondale. Even Gaines had never met him, they'd only spoken over the phone.

After having the opportunity to speak with Roberts at length that evening, he offered me a job at the White House on the vice president's Advance staff. Within two weeks my bags were packed and I was headed for DC. Not only had I not finished college, my skin hadn't even cleared up.

(Coincidentally, when I arrived back at my apartment the day after the Carbondale event, anxious to tell my roommate that I'd just had possibly the best night of my life, certainly the most propitious, it turned out my roommate had also had possibly the best night of his life the night before. He'd attended a wedding reception and met two women who ended up taking him home and seducing him. That was about as common an occurrence to us as being offered a job on the White House staff. At the time I was certain that my previous evening's experience had more meaning, more long-term benefit than his. I could have been wrong.)

When I arrived at the White House, at the Old Executive Office Building, with luggage in-hand, it was a warm June Saturday. My new boss, Bill Roberts, had suggested we meet when I arrive. The first people I saw as I walked through the gate were Hamilton Jordan and Zbigniew Brzezinski standing outside the door to the West Wing, chatting. It hadn't escaped me that I was still just a punk, but I was a punk working at the White House.

Jump ahead to the Carter/Mondale re-election campaign in 1980. I led an Advance team for First Lady Roselynn Carter in Milwaukee for a set of events that included a RON (Remain Over Night) at the Pfister Hotel. A couple of days into the Advance, the hotel manager came to me and asked if I knew anyone with the Humphry presidential campaign from 1968 because they had left some large unpaid bills and the manager still wanted to see if he could get them paid. He had kept them all of those years and obviously never forgot. Before I checked out, I visited the manager a final time to be certain our billing arrangements were satisfactory.

Earlier that same year, in January 1980, I led a team for Vice President Mondale in Iowa that included a RON at the Terrace Inn, a motel facing Interstate 80 outside of Newton. The Terrace Inn was a nice, regular motel with single rooms. No suites. We needed a suite for the vice president.

I was able to convince the Inn's owners that our need for a suite was so great that they offered to set up two connecting rooms as a suite, using their daughter and son-in-law's brand-new living room furniture, including a couch, lounge chairs, a bar, lamps and tables. The daughter and son-in-law lived a couple miles down the road, and the night before the vice president's arrival we went there with a flatbed truck and hauled all of it to the motel. They threw-in some artwork and vases with flowers to go with it. The vice president and his traveling staff had no idea that it wasn't a normal suite until we told them. They all made it a point to thank the Inn's owners and their family.

Then we left town.

Eight years later, just prior to the Iowa caucuses of 1988, as I drove east on Interstate 80 out of Des Moines doing an Advance trip for Dick Gephardt's presidential campaign, I saw the Terrace Inn and pulled off to say hello. As I walked-in the front door, before I could approach or say a word, the lady behind the desk said, "I remember you. You were with Vice President Mondale," and it was a very happy greeting. After eight freaking years.

It was one of those moments, of which there are thousands when you're doing Advance, where you're glad you didn't leave blood. It probably helped that we paid our bills.

CHAPTER 2

Litton Memorial Dinner, Kansas City 1976;
Someone Forced to Get Stoned by Bullies

The names in this essay have been changed to protect the guilty, for reasons that will become obvious. I promised complete anonymity to the parties involved until after they're dead, which, fortunately, hasn't happened. The youngest member of the advance team, Ship, is still vigorous and virile and active. Some say even handsome. The two old pros, Larry and Gill, should probably be in the Old Advance Person's Home (formerly the Old Advance Man's Home), but no one wants to tell them.

The following well-documented advance trip was related to me in detail contemporaneously by the participants.

I knew Collin Shipley well. Still do. The people on the campaign called him Ship. He was twenty-one years old, in the fourth semester of his sophomore year in college because he kept dropping out to work in political campaigns. Despite his experience in politics, he had a bad case of imposter syndrome.

He'd been hired on Jimmy Carter's national advance staff by people he assumed knew what they were doing, and he certainly wasn't going to say no. Just as certainly he was trying his best not to do anything completely stupid.

Ship also assumed that everyone else on the campaign, all of whom seemed older, wiser and more experienced, were more competent than he. He came to realize as time passed that it wasn't necessarily true. A lot of time had to pass before he came to that realization.

It was only his sixth advance trip and he was returning to Kansas City, familiar territory, to do the advance for Governor Carter's visit in October 1976. For Ship it was a deeply emotional assignment.

The primary purpose of the visit was Carter's appearance at a memorial dinner to honor the late Congressman Jerry Litton, who had died in a plane crash with his wife Sharon and their two children two months earlier— the night of the Missouri primary election in which Jerry won his biggest victory to secure the Democratic nomination for U.S. Senate.

Litton was also the first public official in Missouri to endorse Carter for president, and Carter felt a debt of gratitude for his early support. It didn't escape the Carter campaign's notice that Missouri was a swing state, and Litton had won in a landslide.

Ship traveled nearly every step of that U.S. Senate campaign with Litton. Originally hired on the Litton staff in February 1976 as deputy campaign manager to organize counties in the central part of the state, he decided to go along with Litton on campaign appearances in those counties, which happened on a constant basis. Ship's first day with Litton lasted nearly twenty-four hours from the moment they left the Chase Park Plaza Hotel in St. Louis to the moment they checked into the Hilton Plaza in Kansas City after campaigning across the state. Ship got about two hours sleep before the next day's campaigning began. Litton didn't seem to mind the fast turnaround. He was tireless, or manic, depending on one's interpretation.

Soon the arrangement became permanent and Ship walked, rode, and flew in tiny little airplanes alongside a truly iconic public servant for the remainder of the campaign until Jerry's death on primary night. Ship earned his keep with regular eighteen-to-twenty-hour days and intense, never let-up campaigning throughout the State of Missouri.

It was a brutal six months; on election night it became surreal and tragic beyond words.

Litton's was a dark horse candidacy in an extreme sense. He had only two percent name recognition state-wide when he started the race in February of that year, and had gone on to win by a huge margin— more than twenty percent—over two better-known candidates. News coverage in Time Magazine called Litton's campaign "the sand lot team that won the World Series."

For Ship the campaign was like sprinting at full speed for weeks, then experiencing the joy of winning, then finding out at the same moment that the finishing line was a solid brick wall, with all the accompanying pain from the sprint and the abrupt stop. The sadness of the Litton family's death was staggering for everyone who knew them.

Happily for Ship, the Carter campaign reached out and hired him on the national advance staff within a month. He viewed it as nothing short of a miracle even though he wasn't especially religious, and less so after Jerry and his family died.

A few weeks later, upon hearing that Governor Carter was scheduled to speak at the memorial dinner, Ship summoned the courage to ask his superiors on the Carter campaign if he could do the advance trip. They kindly agreed.

Ship expected nothing special beyond the poignance of the dinner, and the fact that it was a presidential campaign and every advance trip was intense. Every trip was memorable, historic, stressful, draining, educational, fun. On some level, every trip carried with it the potential for disaster. But the Kansas City advance added new things to the mix. It was also weird and frenzied and frightening as hell, and ultimately successful.

Immediately following an advance trip to southern California, Ship arrived in KC on Monday, October 11, four days before the dinner on Friday. He checked-in to the historic Hotel Muehlebach, Harry Truman's old haunt, where the memorial dinner was to be held. The "lead" advance, Larry Nichols, and press advance, Gill Bower, were expected early in the afternoon. They didn't arrive.

Ship, surprised and confused about their non-appearance, cooled his heels for the next 20 hours waiting for word about his two advance team colleagues. Headquarters had no idea where they were.

The next day around noon they sauntered-in, laughing and yucking it up as they walked down the hotel hallway, obviously enjoying Ship's confusion and their own mini-rebellion against the dictates of the Carter campaign. They were intent on arriving when *they* thought they needed to arrive and not a moment sooner.

Then it began. Larry and Gill had their own agenda, which Ship assumed had been honed from months of close collaboration. At the ages of 29 and 28 they were old guys; totally self-confident, completely in-charge, mustachioed and hip and clearly enjoying their roles as advance men for the Democratic presidential nominee.

The moment they dropped their luggage in their rooms they asked Ship if he knew of an office supply store nearby. They swooped him up, made him drive Larry's rental car (they sat in the back seat), and headed out to buy supplies for a staff office they would create in the hotel. Gill was carrying over $10,000 in campaign vouchers— in $25, $50 and $100 denominations—essentially cash. Larry's voucher-writing privileges had been suspended by headquarters because he hadn't submitted his receipts from his last five trips. He was instructed to hand over his stash of vouchers to Gill.

They made a haul at the office supply store, buying boxes of pens, mechanical pencils, magic markers, stationary, file folders, scotch tape and other usual office items. They also bought several items, such as mini-tape recorders, a couple cameras, film, flashlights and, oddly, a turntable to play records. It came as a surprise to see the office supply store was selling audio components, and Gill saw it as a boon.

When Gill spotted the turntables he practically jumped. "We need one of those," he said, clearly delighted. "Luxury goods!" Just as clearly, most of the larger purchases would be going home with Larry and Gill after the advance trip.

In the days before computerized, itemized receipts, a salesclerk could merely write "office supplies" on a tear-off pad and it served as documentation.

Larry and Gill enjoyed their shopping excursion. Their glee was infectious. Ship could only imagine how many times that scene had played-out in their previous advance trips. He thought, "In 1980, when I'm doing leads in the presidential re-election campaign, I'm going to make out like a bandit." (As it turned-out, by the time 1980 rolled around and Ship was one of the old hands on the staff, at times carrying more than $20,000 in vouchers, he never made an office supply run such as that. At one point he bought an umbrella for a trip he did for the First Lady and kept it, but that was the extent of his campaign larceny.)

After a little conversation and some off-hand remarks, Larry and Gill basically admitted that they needed to go home between advance trips to deposit their most recent purchases of ill-gotten booty before hitting the road again, which was why they were late in arriving in Kansas City. Nobody needs to travel with boxes of office equipment and supplies when all of it, and more, can be purchased anew in the next town.

Larry said they were doing their part to help the local economy.

Arriving back at the Hotel Muehlebach, Larry instructed Ship to park immediately outside the front door, in the short-term parking zone, where he could get to the car at a moment's notice. Gill parked his rental car there too, and the next day when Ship got a car, he followed suit. The advance team claimed exclusive parking privileges and no one seemed to mind.

The next few hours were a whirl of phone calls to campaign headquarters in Atlanta, coordinating with local contacts, finding vendors and securing volunteers, setting-up the staff office in a hotel room that connected with Larry's, then doing site visits downstairs to the Muehlebach Grand Ballroom to meet the memorial dinner organizers, and then, finally, late in the afternoon, to North Kansas City to find a site for a large campaign rally they were tasked with producing. Carter was scheduled to go directly to the rally as soon as he arrived on the afternoon of the 15th.

Larry and Gill were clearly pros. They showed not a moment's hesitation; they appeared to know exactly what needed to be accomplished and in what order. Ship's first impressions of the two oldsters had not been kind, but he was quickly changing his mind. Both were brilliant in their own ways, and it was clear they *thought* they were the smartest guys in the room no matter the room. Conspicuous self-confidence seemed to be an asset in the world of advance.

Ship had already learned that the mantra of advance is "control." Everyone must know who is in charge, everyone must accept who is in charge, and the advance people in charge must live up to the challenge every single time. And importantly, in the end, everyone who interacts with the advance team should have had a positive experience. Carter/Mondale advance staffers were specifically instructed never to "leave blood" because sooner or later the candidate would have to return to that town, and a greeting committee full of pissed-off local citizenry was not the "visual" that the campaign wanted to see on TV.

Larry and Gill were definitely in control.

Then it happened.

As the three advance guys were driving back to the hotel from the site that Larry and Gill had chosen for the rally, with Ship at the wheel, Larry, from the back seat, mentioned the time.

"It's six o'clock," he said. Ship glanced into the rearview mirror to look at Larry, who continued, "Cocktail time."

At that, Larry pulled a joint out of his shirt pocket and held it up.

Ship declined before it was even offered. "Oh no, I can just see it now—a headline on the bottom of page fifty-two of the New York Times that reads, 'Carter Advance Punk Arrested for Pot Possession in Missouri' followed by me losing my job."

It wasn't as if he hadn't tried pot before. It was the '70s and he was still in college. But he never would have considered doing it when he was working in previous political campaigns, so it follows that he wouldn't as he was beginning his journey on the national advance staff in his first presidential campaign.

Gill interjected, "Come on, what are the chances?"

"Yeah," Larry said. "The New York Times would never cover anything that happens in Missouri."

Ship thought that was relatively clever, but not clever enough to warrant Larry's self-satisfaction with the quip.

Gill had to add the old, "Come on, it will relax you. You're too uptight."

Ship showed surprising resolve for one so overwhelmed by old guys and so eager to be accepted. "Yeah, I used that line with girls in high school, but I was pushing beer. I'll tell you what they all told me— 'I think I prefer uptight right now.'"

Larry lit the joint and took a couple long tokes, then handed it to Gill, still sitting next to him in the back seat. Gill took one puff then offered it to Ship. Ship was having none of it. Gill and Larry passed it back and forth a couple of times and then Larry threw the ragged end out of the window. Ship was appalled. Where he came from, the people who smoked pot would have saved that ragged end. The act pegged Larry as a cavalier bohemian in Ship's mind.

"Back to work," Larry said when they pulled into their reserved parking space in front of the hotel.

Back to work it was. Larry and Gill were seemingly unaffected. There was no "Wow, man, far out, I'm wasted" about it. No sitting around in a daze.

The evening schedule was critical. It included the team's first countdown meeting with their Secret Service counterparts, followed by a conference "trip call" with national staff at headquarters, followed by a meeting with hotel staff— specifically the Muehlebach's sales manager, Inga. She was responsible for all the details required by their special VIP guest as well as our requirements for fifty or sixty members of the traveling press corps.

Larry and Gill ran the meetings and engaged everyone in a glib but professional manner. Even the Secret Service advance lead was impressed, despite the fact that Larry and Gill purposely dressed like bums. They knew their subject matter and were as upbeat and productive as they'd been all afternoon. It occurred to Ship that maybe they were stoned then too. He had no idea.

Apparently they also weren't afflicted with the munchies. By 9 p.m. Ship was famished, and no one had spoken a word about dinner. He finally asked if anyone would like a sandwich from the Haberdashery, a bar and grill underneath the Muehlebach, so named because Harry Truman's haberdashery was located across the street during the 1920s.

As Ship walked outside onto Wyandotte Street then around the hotel to 12th Street to reach the Haberdashery, he was surprised by the level of activity. He noticed it was mostly women in high heels.

Several ladies of the evening were plying their trade in his immediate vicinity, and Ship felt a little daunted. He morphed down from feeling "normal"— like a 15-year-old— to feeling like a 12-year-old. A vulnerable one.

Naturally, he was approached by two ladies who looked experienced, way-experienced, and his only thought was, "What the hell am I going to say?" He really, really didn't want to seem rude.

For some happy reason, just as the women spoke the words "Hey sweetheart, you're a cutie, would you like a date?" Ship remembered a line he heard on a TV show, "I'd love to ladies, but I can't afford you."

They laughed and walked by after one responded, "Too bad, I could make you happy."

"Thank you though," Ship said as he scooted away. It seemed like the polite thing to say.

Walking back up 12th Street with the sandwiches, he wondered how it would look when Carter spent the night on Friday with the hotel surrounded by hookers.

The team ate at 10 p.m. and stopped working at midnight. Ship was exhausted from the pace and the work and the energy he'd expended to keep up with all the witty repartee.

Day 2, Which Should Have Been Day 3

The next morning began with a staff meeting at 8 a.m. and a meeting at 8:15 with the first two volunteers who'd been recruited to work in the staff room. The number would grow almost hourly as the advance progressed.

Larry informed Ship that he would be responsible for the entire Muehlebach site, which included the dinner and a "pool spray" that was scheduled for around 10 p.m. After the memorial dinner, the national and local press pool would be escorted into Carter's room to get video/photos of him watching the vice presidential debate between Walter Mondale, Carter's running mate, and Bob Dole, the Republican nominee for VP.

The assignment also meant that Ship would lead Carter for the first time—down to the dinner and back—using a maze of service elevators and back hallways and a route through the hotel's kitchen. Ship immediately thought of Robert Kennedy and the Ambassador Hotel in 1968, and the thought remained with him.

At 9 a.m. Ship met with Inga and the Litton Memorial Dinner organizers to formalize the site plan that he'd sketched the night before— with press parking and access, candidate/public/press logistics, room layout, check-in tables, holding room, staging and production— and provide the hotel and the production vendors with a final plan.

Ship was beginning to feel he might be starting to grasp his responsibilities for the advance trip when he went back upstairs to the staff office at 10 a.m. and reported to Larry, who was pleased with the progress Ship made in sewing up the memorial dinner. Ship was ready to begin helping with the rally, which required more in terms of messaging, visuals, site preparation, crowd building, press accommodations, volunteers and public interaction.

Larry had specific ideas. "Gill is going to need you to help him with local press because you already have a relationship there, and we need some news coverage to build our crowd. And he needs you to find a radio station where we can record an ad for the rally."

"Shouldn't be a problem," Ship said.

Larry continued, "But I need you to go out to the airport first to pick up a Delta Dash from headquarters."

It was a straightforward request, spoken matter-of-factly. In the days before FedEx and overnight delivery, Delta Airlines had a service where you could deliver your package to the airport and they would fly it on one of their passenger planes to a destination airport, where the receiving party would pick it up. Quite futuristic.

Ship didn't ask what it was, he just toddled off to KCI (also known as "Kansas City Inconvenience") like a good little advance team member. The large, fat, envelope, with a return sticker officially printed "Carter-Mondale 1976 Presidential Campaign" was waiting at the Delta package counter.

An hour later he arrived back at the hotel and toddled up to the staff office to find Larry. One of the volunteers told Ship that he'd gone next door to his room, so Ship knocked on the door. Larry was surprisingly happy to see him. He invited Ship in, then closed the door behind him.

Ship handed the package to Larry who, without saying a word, tore it open. Inside was a large plastic baggie with a large amount of pot.

Ship surged through the seven stages of shock to anger within a nanosecond. "How much is in there?" he asked, "How much was I carrying around?"

"Only about a quarter pound," Larry said, followed by a shit-eating grin.

"So, just to be clear, I was your mule," Ship said, not smiling. "Seems a little rude not to mention it to me ahead of time, a lot of which I could've been spending in Leavenworth just up the road."

"You had plausible deniability," Larry said.

"THAT would have done me a lot of good," Ship said as he walked out of Larry's room and back into the staff office. He made it a point not to talk to Larry for the next several hours. Larry didn't notice.

Needless to say, the "It's cocktail time" scenario played out again that evening as they were once again driving back from the rally site where they'd met with Secret Service and the production crew. Once again, Ship declined.

Once again Larry and Gill pressed the issue. The joint they were passing looked fatter to Ship than the one the day before. He knew why.

At 6:30 they arrived back at the Muehlebach and attended their second countdown meeting with the Secret Service to review the schedule and coordinate logistical issues. Larry, sitting at a table at the head of the conference room alongside his Secret Service counterpart, the lead Secret Service advance, was still on his A-game. If he was "altered" in any way it didn't show.

The evening was as frenetic and productive as the evening before as crowd building for the rally took priority. The staff office was buzzing with volunteers making phone calls, creating press passes and making hand-made signs to post in key locations. Ship hooked-up Larry with one of the local labor unions and Larry arranged for them to phone bank to union members throughout the region.

Ship arranged a visit with Gill to a local soft-rock radio station and cut a 60-second ad. Gill carried a recording of the Carter campaign song ("They said his name was Jimmy Carter and he was running for President . . ."), which he used at the beginning and the end of the ad. "Come see Jimmy Carter this Friday afternoon" he announced with punch of a carnival barker. Within an hour they had a half-dozen copies of the 60-second ad, and by the end of the night four radio stations were playing it. As Gill and Ship arrived back at the Muehlebach they heard the soft-rock station air it. Immediate marketing promotion.

Also in the air—and on the sidewalk when Ship and Gill arrived at 9:30—was the ambiance of Kansas City downtown hospitality. Ship recognized the two ladies he'd spoken with the night before, and they him. They waved to him. "Hi there, cutie."

"Hello ladies. Be careful out there," Ship called back.

Gill stood back and looked at Ship, who simply smiled.

They worked until midnight again before knocking-off. Once again Ship was exhausted even though he was having fun, except for the part where his lead tricked him into carrying enough contraband to send him up the river for twenty years.

Day 3, Which Should Have Been day 4

The next morning broke too early.

After the 8 a.m. staff and 8:30 volunteer meetings, Ship met with Inga to advance the hotel suite that the Muehlebach management had chosen and named in Jerry Litton's honor for Carter's use. In the spirit of "no detail is too small," Ship needed to see it himself.

One potential problem loomed. Carter preferred single hotel rooms. No suites. Regular rooms. Apparently, he was quite adamant about it, according to the advance office.

However, it was the night of the vice presidential debate between Walter Mondale, the good guy, and Bob Dole, Nixon's attack dog. As a result, they needed a room large enough to accommodate a large press pool with cameras to shoot video of Carter watching the debate. They needed more space than any single room could provide, but it had to "look like a normal room," according to Larry.

Ship and Inga met in the lobby and took the elevator up to the sixth floor. Affixed to the door was an engraved brass plate with the words "The Jerry Litton Suite" in a tasteful script. Ship figured he could cover it just before the pool spray with a sign that read "Press Pool," and then rip that down after the press departed.

The suite was lovely. Immediately upon entering Ship was greeted with a glass panel that separated the entryway and the living area, and on it was a beautifully painted scene of water sprites, or nymphs, or whatever cavorts in an ocean mostly naked. There were breasts and everything.

The staff at headquarters was sensitive about the whole sex thing since Carter famously admitted to "lusting in his heart." And of course Ship personally did not want to be responsible for any unintended lusting triggers.

"Uhhhhhhh" Ship said. "This may be a problem, Inga. We have to bring press in here to watch Governor Carter watching the vice presidential debate on Friday night, and unless we can remove this, we'll have to find another suite."

Inga seemed surprised. "Why? This is lovely, and tasteful," she said in her clipped Swedish accent.

"I agree, but the staff will have a problem with it, and they will fire me, so . . ."

"You wouldn't be offended to see me like this, would you?" Inga asked.

Ship wasn't expecting that. Inga was in her 30s, and very pretty, and tall and lithe and very Nordic, and very business-like. He had no idea how to respond. He couldn't even remember lines from a TV show to fill-in. "Uhhhhh, no?," he stuttered.

Then he recovered, grinned and looked at her. "OK," his right eyebrow raised, "maybe a little."

She got the joke and laughed for the first time since he'd met her. "This is good," she said, "we will have to talk about this further."

Ship agreed. "I'd like that, but first, can you show me another suite? A boring one that I can fit fifteen people into, preferably on this floor?"

"I believe I have exactly what you need," she said.

"That wouldn't surprise me at all," he said. She laughed again.

Luckily, she had another suite immediately opposite of the Litton Suite, originally intended for the Secret Service detail leader. Inga could swap those rooms, and Service wouldn't have to change accommodations on the floors above and below.

Disaster averted.

They rode down to the lobby in the elevator together and Inga offered her hand. "Thank you. I look forward to talking with you later about appropriate bathing attire."

"Thank *you*," Ship said, "and, uhhh, thank you."

She smiled again, raised an eyebrow, and walked away.

Ship was feeling pretty good. Pretty confident. Pretty invincible. Advance was a good thing.

Larry and Ship headed out to the hardware store for another economy-enhancing purchase, this time of site supplies in bulk— ropes, stakes, duct tape, staple guns, cardboard, caution tape, several colors of spray paint, regular paint, paint brushes, super glue. "Super glue?" Ship asked Larry. "Why Super Glue?"

"You never know when it'll come in handy," he said diabolically.

They then went to the rally site for a walk-thru with the Secret Service site agents, then visited a labor union hall where Gill had organized a poster painting party, ostensibly for volunteers to paint rally signs but also for the purpose of getting some free press coverage. He invited local TV stations' news crews to cover the event in preparation for Governor Carter's visit.

Ship delivered the stacks of white cardboard and paints, and soon Gill's army of volunteers were painting signs. Over the next half hour, three of Kansas City's TV stations' news crews arrived for the event. Gill gave interviews (he'd shaved his continuous three-day growth of beard) and was clearly in his element.

They then headed back to the hotel for their 6:30 countdown meeting.

Along the way, with Ship at the wheel and Larry in the front seat, it was "cocktail time" again. Larry lit a blunt and took a puff then offered it to Ship. This time Ship took it. "What the hell," he said. He inhaled deeply, the inhalation of a deeply confident young man.

Larry was tickled and amused, but everything tickled and amused him, so it wasn't a special occasion. They each took a couple more puffs before Larry threw out the roach. Ship was still functional for the countdown meeting and the evening's work. No big deal, but the BLT on whole wheat toast that he ate that night, which Ship insisted on being no later than 8 o'clock because HE was hungry, tasted especially good.

At 11 p.m., Larry, Ship and three volunteers drove out to KCI to pick up rental cars for the motorcade, specifically one van for the staff and three station wagons with drop-down tail gates and luggage racks for the network camera crews. Camera men (an all-male profession at the time) would stand or kneel out of the back of the station wagon, hang on the luggage rack, and film the motorcade as it drove. It was called "the body watch," in case something happened the governor's person, such as a crash or bullets. Lovely.

As they waited at the Avis Rental counter, Larry noticed a young woman standing in the Hertz counter nearby in the mostly deserted airport, hunched over a cross word puzzle. He sauntered over to her. She was trying to do the New York Times crossword and not faring well.

"May I try?" Larry asked.

"Sure" she said and handed it to him.

He took a pen out of his shirt pocket and started reading the clues. Then he stared writing. He continued writing.

Ship sauntered over. The girl at the Hertz counter looked at him. She looked incredulous. "Is he kidding?" she asked.

"I don't think so," Ship said.

Larry finished the puzzle and handed it back to her. He was clearly tickled and amused.

Neat trick, Ship thought.

They arrived back at the hotel and broke for the night at 1 a.m. It was a productive day. Their poster party event made the 10 o'clock news on all four channels, thousands of leaflets had been produced and distributed to volunteer teams, hundreds of phone calls had been made, radio stations were calling for interviews with Gill and Larry, all the logistics were falling into place and Ship had no idea what had happened that morning with Inga, but he felt good about it.

Game Day: Day 4, Which Should Have Been Day 5

He woke up thinking, "What was that thing with Inga?" Then the day's events consumed him.

It was planned to the minute. The advance team's schedule called for all of them to depart the hotel at 2:30 p.m. to meet Carter's airplane. Ship would drive Larry and Gill in his rental car and lead their own motorcade consisting of the staff van and station wagons, driven by volunteers, to the Downtown Airport for a 4:00 wheels-down. The plan called for Ship to pick up a volunteer driver at the airport, then upon wheels-down, get Carter's press secretary, Jody Powell, and drive with him back to the Muehlebach while Larry and Gill traveled with Carter to the rally. Simple enough.

Powell wanted to go straight to the hotel from the airport, and Ship needed to be back at the hotel to oversee the speech-site prep, make sure Carter's suite was re-arranged for the evening's pool spray, and lead Carter into the hotel from the motorcade on arrival. Upon arriving at Carter's suite with the governor, it would then be Ship's duty to explain why he had a luxury suite and not a single, average, room.

Larry, Gill, and Ship were the rally site at 7 a.m. to meet with contractors and volunteers. Ship arrived back at the hotel at 9 a.m. to meet with his memorial dinner counterparts and Inga for a final walk-through.

Ship went back to the rally site to help with the "build" mostly because he didn't want to be seen as trying to weedle out of the back-busting manual labor, as much as he wanted to weedle out of it, then back to the Muehlebach to change clothes and oversee the ballroom set-up. He wanted to ensure that the press area was built so both local and national press had access to the ballroom and the dinner without being a major disruption, which could easily happen in a somber setting.

Ship was back in the staff office at 2:15, as Larry asked, for a brief meeting before their 2:30 departure. Gill and Larry walked in shortly after and all three went into Larry's room.

Larry looked concerned but had a solution to his worried state of mind. It was cocktail time again.

Ship shouldn't have been surprised, but was. Once again he was firm in his resolve. "Nope, not if you held a gun to my head. Well maybe if you held a gun to my head, but I don't think you geezer delinquents carry those," Ship said.

"You *have* to," Larry said, "it will help relax you and it's a tradition. We always take a toke or two before the event."

Gill interjected, "Here, I'll take one." He held it to his mouth, sucked, handed it back to Larry and turned away. Ship would find out months later that he literally had not inhaled. He blew it out immediately because he knew that it wasn't the same stuff they'd smoked the day before. It was Martian weed or some other kind of exotic, overly-potent mind-altering herb.

Larry insisted. "You did fine with it yesterday, go ahead, enjoy the moment."

Ship experienced an interesting mix of intimidation and invincibility. He was wearing a suit, looking together, feeling the feeling. He took the joint from Larry and took a puff. He made the mistake of inhaling. It took him off-guard and he coughed, but he attributed the harsh burning in his lungs for the fact that he was inhaling smoke. He refused another.

Larry gave him the day's staff pin, or "S" pin, to wear on his lapel. It was a Secret Service "day pin" made from tin with a bend-over tab. They were made in different colors for different trips so the Service could identify who was "staff"; in other words, "those allowed to be close to the protectee." The lead and the staff that traveled with Carter had permanent, or "hard" staff pins.

As he drove to the airport, only ten minutes away from the hotel across the Broadway bridge, Ship could sense something was different. His head was in another time zone, on another planet. By the time Peanut One landed and Governor Carter deplaned, as they say, Ship was in full-blown paranoiac meltdown. The magnitude of his simple, mindless responsibilities overwhelmed him, and he believed, he believed in his soul as he'd never believed anything in his life, that everyone *knew* he was stoned. Everyone could smell it, or see it, or sense it, and everyone was not happy about it.

Jody Powell came off the plane looking for his ride after the motorcade departed and Ship, wearing the obligatory advance man trench coat, escorted him to the car. Ship was forced to sit in the back seat with Jody because the driver had brought another volunteer who wanted to return to the Muehlebach. It was agony; Ship was certain that Powell could tell he was stoned.

The ten-minute trip lasted hours. Ship could not look in Powell's direction. He spoke only when Powell spoke to him, only enough to explain how the logistics for the pool spray would work, and he did it poorly.

Powell must have thought Ship was odd in some way, although he may not have noticed at all. He'd immediately cracked a window and lit up a cigarette for the journey, so Ship's "smell" would not have been an issue, if he could have thought rationally.

Back at the hotel, in preparing for Carter's arrival, Ship neglected to remove his trench coat, ever. He was beside himself with paranoia with a capital NOI. He avoided the Secret Service site agents, he avoided the Litton Memorial Dinner organizers, he avoided the hotel staff, he avoided Inga, he didn't go to his room, he never took off his trench coat.

His security "S" pin was on the lapel of his suit jacket underneath his trench coat, which would not be a problem for the Secret Service agents with whom he worked that week and knew him by sight. However, none of the of the Carter Detail, the traveling Secret Service Agents, had seen him enough know who he was.

Ship didn't think of that detail about the Detail because he hadn't noticed the extra piece of clothing he was wearing for no good reason. He was a worried man. Whatever he did, he was certain it wouldn't be right, and everyone would know it was because he was stoned, and they would judge him harshly.

In just a short time Ship would have to explain to Governor Carter why they were standing in the middle of a cavernous, wood paneled suite instead of a dank little single with a queen size bed. All Ship could think was "He will know I'm stoned. He will know. He will know."

An hour and a half later nothing had changed his altered paranoiac state and Ship was tasked with meeting the motorcade and leading Carter to the elevator and to his room.

As the motorcade pulled up outside the Muehlebach's 12th Street entrance, Ship positioned himself near the door, holding his clipboard with two green "Carter for President" bumper stickers pasted on the back. Carter's leads had a system whereby Carter could find them in a crowd when they held up a clipboard with the bumper stickers on the back.

A large group of Carter supporters were waiting at the barricades—small sawhorses—just feet from the limo and Carter. The sawhorses shifted and people walked through, and the agents had to push their way through the crowd. Ship, standing just outside the hotel doors, held up the clipboard and Carter made his way toward him. Ship then led him through the door and down the hallway toward the elevator, which was being held by an agent and a hotel employee. Ship stepped back to allow Carter to enter first. Carter's assistant, Greg Schneiders, was already inside. Ship entered next, then approximately five hundred Secret Service agents piled in and Ship was pressed like a sardine to one side.

None of the agents recognized Ship and none could see his pin, cleverly hidden under his trench coat. The doors closed and the elevator buzzed because it was overloaded. The doors opened and one of the agents closest to the outside backed out. The doors closed again and it rose. Ship noticed a couple of the agents, or it may have been all the agents, were giving him the once-over twice. They were eyeballing him up and down. Ship assumed the worst, not that he was wearing his security pin where no one could see it, but that everyone could see or smell or sense that he was stoned. Ssstttoonnneddd. All the agents HAD to know.

Then Ship looked up, and standing a few feet away, as the maze of heads and bodies separated slightly, was Jimmy Carter's face, and he was looking straight at him.

Ship was dumbstruck with the thought, *"Oh crap, he knows. Be cool, just be cool. Oh crap he knows, he can tell."* He was frozen. *"Be cool, just be cool. How they hell do I do that?"*

These were the thoughts racing through Ship's mind at that moment, as it was related to me.

Ship had no answers, only aspirations. The thought, *"Be cool"* once again danced on the decision-making part of his brain, which opted for *"Act like an idiot."*

Ship looked at the governor and grinned, with corners of his mouth raised, and raised his eyebrows to go along with it. It was a stupid-looking grin. Ship knew it when he did it.

Carter looked at Ship for a moment, looked slightly down and away for a nano-second, then looked back at Ship and smiled a courteous but genuine smile.

To Ship it was a knowing smile, a wry, insightful, knowing smile.

"That's it. He knows. He knows. I'm gonna be fired." Ship's mind broke. He couldn't look to see if Carter was still looking at him. Ship was supposed to get out of the elevator and lead him to the suite and give him "the explanation."

Instead, when the elevator reached the sixth floor and the doors opened, Ship remained inside as the other occupants, including Carter, exited. Ship was not leading; he was following the pack. He figured that the Secret Service wouldn't let Carter get lost.

By the time Ship entered the suite behind everyone else, Carter was walking out of one large room on the left, through the living area, into and out of another large room on the right. He then walked over near Ship, and Ship didn't wait to be asked; he lurched into his "spiel."

"Wellgovernorthereasonwehavethissuiteisbecauseofthevicepresidentialdebateandweneedtobringinapresspooltowatchyouwatchingtelevisionat9p.m.andifyouneedmeyouknowwheretofindme" and boom, he turned and walked out the door. He didn't wait to see if Carter or anyone else reacted.

He knew his career as a presidential campaign advance man was kaput.

As the next hour and a half passed, Ship slowly returned to earth but he remained convinced that the damage was irreparable.

He had a chance to walk outside for a few minutes, to regroup and get a breath of fresh downtown Kanas City air. When he did, he noticed that that scene was eerily quiet. With the exception of security personnel near the motorcade, there was no one on the streets, even outside the security perimeter.

Ship walked over to one of the Kansas City policemen, a sergeant, and asked him what happened to all the night life.

"We asked the ladies who normally work down here to find another location for the evening, considering our special guest and the increased police presence," the sergeant explained. "We didn't think it was a good look for the city."

"They were looking forward to entertaining the traveling press," Ship said. "This could have made those ladies' month. I hope you feel badly about it."

"I do," he explained, "but what could I do about it. I just take orders."

It was a valuable lesson for Ship. It was the Kansas City Police Department as an extension of the Chamber of Commerce.

After Secret Service bomb teams swept the grand ballroom and secured it, the memorial dinner crowd began filing in. "Pre-set" for local and national press camera crews was accomplished smoothly. All the volunteers were accomplishing their jobs spectacularly, the hotel staff was happy, the Secret Service was happy, Larry and Gill were happy, as usual, and Ship was morose. He had to go upstairs and face Carter again, and then lead him down to the dinner at the appointed time.

Once again, Ship could comprehend the simple task of walking in front of another human being and talking. Just as the burden was lifting from Ship's mind, Larry and Gill suggested they go back to Larry's room before the dinner. Ship had a two-word reply, one of which was a four-letter obscenity.

They were tickled and amused, again. Their suggestion wasn't so much an attempt to pressure him as it was to taunt him for being stupid enough to trust Larry the first time.

Ship repeated his four-letter aria a few times in close proximity to both of their faces, to emphasize the point, then left to go up one floor to Carter's suite. When he entered, he was relieved to see Greg Schneiders talking with Governor Carter. Ship's only words were, "They're ready downstairs whenever you are, sir." Carter and Schneiders talked as they walked and Ship kept his distance. Magically, the walk to the service elevator, through the service corridor and the kitchen to another service hallway behind the grand ballroom, went without a hitch. Ship had regained the ability to walk and think almost simultaneously without sweating through his nice clean suit.

Carter was introduced to the podium fairly quickly after he arrived, as per the dinner organizers' agreement with Ship, and it appeared at first that Carter's remarks would be less than appropriate. He opened with a few humorous comments about the baseball team and Kansas City barbeque and some other innocuous Kansas City-based concepts and Ship thought it might be a disaster.

No one who knows Jimmy Carter would have thought that thought.

Soon, with the quiet sincerity of a small-town preacher, Carter began to speak of the life of Congressman Litton. Without notes, he detailed the challenges and accomplishments that shaped Jerry's life since childhood. He recounted episodes from Jerry's college years, his business life and his political career, and he spoke of Jerry's family in touching terms. Jerry's mother and father, Mildred and Charlie, were in the audience. It was a moving speech and an emotional evening.

When Carter sat down after an extended standing ovation, he pushed back in his chair to look behind those seated at the dais, and he glanced to his right and left looking for his advance man. When he looked left, he saw Ship standing at the end of the platform, indicating it was the direction Carter should depart.

Ship caught Carter's eye. Carter leaned back slightly, raised his right-hand stomach-high, and gave Ship a slight "howdy," two small up and down movements with his fingers, to let him know that he'd seen him.

At that moment Ship knew everything was O.K.

Carter, Ship, and the Secret Service detail were soon making their way back through the bowels of the Muehlebach to the suite. Ship thanked him for the wonderful speech as they walked, explaining that he'd worked closely with Jerry, and Carter offered a few more remarkable insights about him. Carter did his homework and remembered everything.

At 9 p.m. Ship helped Gill wrangle the press pool for the pool spray in the suite, as Carter watched Mondale and Dole duke it out. Once again Gill was in his element with the press, always happy and always one step ahead of any concerns they might express. Ship learned a lot by watching him.

At 9:10 the press pool was ushered out and Gill decided that he and Ship should remain and watch the rest of the debate with Jimmy, Jody, and Greg. He had brass balls. Ship stood and watched for about

10 minutes before quietly leaving because he didn't want to be seen as a "clutch." Gill had no such qualms.

The Litton campaign staff reunion started in the lobby bar after the dinner and continued until after 1 a.m. Mere weeks had passed since they busted their butts together in the cause of getting Jerry elected. All were young, none were grizzled campaign veterans; they'd been left with a feeling of emptiness afterward that was impossible to grasp, and they alone shared it.

Ship peeled himself away from his friends at 1:30 and ambled slowly back to his room, where he peeled off his clothes and took the best hot shower in his entire life. He slept the sleep of the innocent but not entirely virtuous.

Day 5, Which Should Have Been Day 6

Saturday morning, the day after, Ship had no responsibilities. He wasn't required to go with the motorcade back to the downtown airport, which departed at 8 a.m., so he slept in until 8:30. The restaurant and lobby were filled with grateful Litton supporters who had attended the dinner and stayed overnight.

Mildred and Charlie Litton saw him as they were leaving the restaurant and they were clearly still emotionally drained. Their appreciation overflowed and they showered it on Ship, who demurred and credited Jimmy Carter and the Carter campaign. Their loss was so unimaginable, everything he said felt weak.

The morning felt good and melancholy at the same time. The end of any advance trip was emotion-laden, a release of anxiety. Ship was finding it took him two days to recover from each trip. He was hoping to spend another day in Kansas City to rest and visit with his new friend Inga.

They met for coffee at 10:30 a.m. and she told him she would be off work at 3 p.m. A nice dinner and a long evening were planned. She arranged for him to move to the suite that Carter didn't use, the Litton suite. The one with the half-naked nymphs cavorting in the foamy sea on the glass room divider. She indicated that she would like to join him, and he was hoping to be cavorting soon himself.

At noon he called the Carter Advance office to talk about his next assignment and the hopes and dreams portion of his world came crashing down. They told him they wanted him on a 4 p.m. flight to Pittsburgh, connecting to a flight to Erie, Pennsylvania, for another advance, and that he'd be working again with Larry and Gill, who would be on the same flights.

Larry and Gill boxed their in-home office supply stores and electronic devices and paid Inga with campaign vouchers to arrange for them to be shipped to their homes.

Ship found Inga in the sales office and told her the bad news. They exchanged phone numbers. He fully expected to make another trip to Kansas City soon and take advantage of the free suite she promised. It never happened.

By the time Ship returned to Kansas City in 1978 to do a trip for Vice President Mondale, Inga had moved on. The White House travel office put Ship in the only other union hotel, the Plaza Hilton, and in the short few minutes he had to inquire at the Muehlebach, he could find no one who was familiar with her.

They never reconnected and he considered it a tragedy of potentially epic proportions.

He had, however, learned some valuable lessons, the first of which was never trust Larry Nichols, whose real name I would divulge if the statute of limitations hadn't expired. Lesson number two was don't smoke that stuff when you're hanging out with the next leader of the free world, or anyone with Secret Service protection for that matter.

The value of the latter is self-evident. The value of the former became increasingly evident as years passed.

South Bend, Indiana,
Summer 1978

Burlington, Vermont,
Fall 1978

Tennessee-Tombigbee Waterway,
Summer 1980

The White House,
Fall 1979

Announcement Day, Iowa Tour, Cedar Rapids, Iowa, February 10, 2007

Clemson University, February 2008; Photo credit: Callie Shell, *Time Magazine*

Gore-Chernomyrdin Commission, Moscow, Russia, December 1994

Brown vs. Board of Education 50th Anniversary, Topeka, Kansas, May, 2004

CHAPTER 3

ADVANCE WOMAN - 1978
VICE PRESIDENTIAL ADVANCE

The women who did presidential-level Advance in the 1970s were pioneers, I just didn't realize it at the time. A dear friend, Kathryn Simmons, was among the first generation to challenge the assumption that only men could be national political operatives, and she was the first to open my eyes about the intense challenges women faced on the road.

Everyone else in the White House advance operation called her Kate, but since she insisted on calling me by my last name, ("Hey, Jakes"!), she was always Simmons to me.

In the Fall of 1978, Kate went to West Virginia as the lead Advance on a White House team to create a set of events for Vice President Mondale's visit, including a rally for local candidates. The V.P.'s office called her at the last minute to fill in for another Advance lead who was forced to cancel due to a death in the family. She was happy to help. However, the last-minute nature of her participation may have led to some confusion among the locals as to the identities of the Advance team members.

Their local contacts were told when to expect the team, with a reference to the "Advance person" who was leading it, before her participation was finalized.

Back in the day, Kate never understood why a male was called an "Advance man" but a female was always referred to as an "Advance person." Maybe it was simply because "Advance woman" didn't trip lightly off the tongue, but "Advance person" certainly wasn't any easier to wrap one's mouth around.

It wasn't a stretch for her to believe that lingering old-timey sexism contributed to the semantic difference even in the enlightened late 1970s. A woman might not be considered the right fit for White House Advance, but a person, what the hell, a person could do it.

She credited Democrats for taking the lead in de-genderfying job titles, and importantly, for breaking the gender barrier of presidential-level political operatives. However, not every Democrat in the land was on-board with that concept from the beginning.

Kate was "Minnesota nice." Flaxen-haired and pretty without making much effort, she was also "Minnesota straight-forward." As I told her once, she was "no-nonsense in the best sense of the term." The daughter of a minister, growing up in a small town, she didn't experience much overt sexism in her youth. Beginning with her first Advance trip, her eyes were opened to the larger reality of sex discrimination.

At a time when the vast majority of Advance staffers were still male, seeing a woman in the role of Lead Advance sometimes landed as a shock to the more conservative elder Democrats with whom she had to work. It happened in every region of the country. She called them the Party's "Neanderthal wing." Happily, they weren't organized. More often than not, after working with Kate, skeptics saw their flawed thinking and prior prejudices dissolve.

This wasn't one of those times.

During her career in Advance, beginning with the 1976 Carter/Mondale campaign, she experienced both subtle and overt sexism several times. As her career progressed it became what she called "a totally unsurprising surprise." Once, in a moment of exasperation after an unnecessarily challenging Advance trip, she told me, "You simply don't expect that crap from fellow Democrats, especially when the White House has sent you to represent the president or the vice president."

The bluntest, most in-your-face attack on her "suitability" as an Advance lead occurred during the trip to West Virginia. It was a four-day Advance—starting on a Tuesday and culminating with a rally on Saturday at noon.

Kate called me shortly after accepting the assignment because she knew I'd worked in the state on a couple advance trips during the '76 campaign. She wanted to know if I knew any of the state Democrats and I was able to provide a few contacts and report that all of the people with whom I'd worked were helpful and generous with their time. My only surprise, I told her, as a fellow Midwesterner, was the openness and ease with which some expressed their feelings about "sensitive" issues, or issues that might be considered controversial, not in a good way.

She told me she understood what I was saying. She also understood, because we had talked about it in the past, that I was speaking from the perspective of a white male. Through our friendship, I learned about how differently women are treated even when they are working in the highest level of government.

I suggested that her first call when she arrived in Charleston should be to a certain Democratic Party official who, as it turned out, would forever be referred to as "Mr. X" because Kate preferred never to speak his name ever again. As it turned out, the V.P.'s Scheduling Office also suggested she contact Mr. X, thank god. It meant I didn't bear sole responsibility.

Upon her arrival on that warm September Tuesday, prior to starting the nitty gritty of producing a major rally in support of Democratic candidates, she went to visit Mr. X for what she thought would be a courtesy call. Under any other circumstance it should have been simple matter -- something along the lines of "This is what we're planning and this is what I need to do it," which is usually met with an enthusiastic "Whatever we can do to help; just let me know." That's the normal conversation when the Lead goes about touching base with the local party bigwigs.

Mr. X had his own ideas due to his keen personal interest in the visit. He'd been lobbying the White House for weeks, asking for both the president and vice president to come to the state early in the general election. This was the first such visit and Mr. X was looking to make a splash.

Kate thought he seemed a little young to be a Neanderthal, even with his shiny bald head. He wore his hair long on the sides in an effort to look younger, or hip, but it didn't work. From the moment Kate arrived he disabused her of the myth of Southern hospitality. He was, to put it mildly, terse, and quite willing to share his feelings. She hadn't even sat yet when he started to spew.

He opened with, "It's obvious that the White House doesn't take this trip seriously. They sent a woman. Not even a woman . . . a girl."

Kate didn't know whether to make light of the comment—treat it as if it were a compliment—or . . . ? Her mind raced.

Then he leaned forward on his desk and his eyes narrowed. "I don't have to take this. I'm gonna get you replaced."

She was stunned, as anyone would be. It took her breath away for a second. As she regrouped the only thing she could think to say was, "You don't even know me."

Mr. X seemed to soften slightly. "It's not personal," he said.

"Seems pretty personal from where I'm sitting," she said. "On the other hand, if you had actually taken the time to work with me *then* decided that I was incompetent, I'd be more upset about it." She knew instinctively that there was no way she was backing-down from this dolt.

She laser-beamed his eyes and continued softly, "I'll tell you what. You make whatever phone calls you need to make and I'll get out of your hair and start doing my job." She meant it as a dig, and she was sure he didn't miss the reference. "I'm sure the White House will let me know how this turns out."

As she stood to leave, she said, "Nice meeting you." Mr. X didn't bother to get up as she walked out.

When she returned to the hotel, the rest of the Advance team, (Joe, Press Advance; Nancy, Site I; Brad, Site II; and Jill, Motorcade), was just arriving. She immediately gathered them in a remote part of the lobby. They could see she was not her usual upbeat self.

"I'd like you to check-in and get settled, then meet me in the staff office, (one of the rooms that she directed the hotel to convert into an office), in a half hour."

Joe Kirmenian, who knew Kate from previous Advance trips, asked if anything was wrong. "Kate, you have a look on your face I've never seen before." She could see *his* concern.

"I didn't think it showed that much," she said. "I apologize. I just had a rather unpleasant experience with our local host, and you should know that he is trying to have me replaced."

Joe jumped to his feet. He was animated but kept his voice low. "What the hell happened? What did he say to you?"

Nancy Kiel, the team's Site 1 and another friend from previous trips, observed dryly, "Let me guess. Were you mean to him, or might it have something to do with you not having a penis?"

"Apparently not having a penis is an unpardonable sin in these parts," Kate said.

Joe was becoming more animated and less quiet. "Screw that guy. If you leave, I'm leaving, and I think we should all leave." The rest of the team concurred.

"Thanks Joe. Let's see what Becky says." Becky Connelly was the director of Scheduling for the vice president, and Kate knew Mr. X's phone call would wind up at her desk sooner or later. "I'll go upstairs and call her."

Ten minutes later she got the answer from Becky that she was hoping for.

Becky's words were wonderful. "Yes, I spoke with him. I told Mr. X that it was up to him," she said. "I informed him that he could either have the vice president visit or not, but if he wanted the vice president, he also wanted the Advance team that we chose to send. He got the message. He doesn't make staffing choices for the White House."

Kate expected no less from Becky. As grateful as she was for her support, it also meant she had to work with that idiot Mr. X or at least be in his vicinity for the next four days.

The Advance team responded to the news of Becky's comments with unrestrained enthusiasm. They sounded like a scene out of 1930s Judy Garland/Mickey Rooney movie musical.

"Then we'll give them the biggest, most astounding campaign rally they've ever seen," Joe said.

Nancy offered "We'll make that sonofabitch eat his words and I want to be there to help shove them down his throat, or in some other orifice." (I doubt Judy Garland used those exact words in any of her movies.)

It was heartwarming for Kate, and much needed. Her initial reaction to Mr. X had been more along the lines of telling him he could do it all himself, or *to* himself, or words to that effect.

The team buckled-down to the task at hand, resolved on avoiding Mr. X to the extent possible. They further resolved to bust their butts to accommodate all of West Virginia's big shots, especially Mr. X's political friends. They wanted everyone with any influence to feel they'd been given the royal treatment. (A dedicated, well-appointed VIP "holding room" with refreshments, and a few well-placed handshakes with the veep, would do the trick. They just had to figure out how to pay for a well-appointed VIP hold with refreshments. Kate had an idea.)

As it turned out, most of the other West Virginia Democrats with whom the team worked were welcoming and helpful. Most.

Kate informed her Secret Service counterpart, Special Agent T.J. Trapasso, of her "dynamic" with the local host. If her political problem turned into a battle of wills either during the Advance or during the VP's visit, it could become a security issue as well, so it was wise to inform him.

T.J. was surprised and supportive. "What, did this guy step back in time fifty years?"

She'd worked with T.J. once before, and while he was unceasingly polite and professional, she wasn't sure about his feelings on the topic of woman Advance leads. Secret Service agents weren't known for being open about their personal views while on the job.

"From our perspective I'd say don't worry about it. We've got your back if he wants to pull any funny stuff," T.J. said. "If he says anything to me about you, I'll let him know what I think, and I won't pull any punches. Rude is rude."

Hearing those words of support lifted her heart. Maybe it was because it meant she had full-throated encouragement from a cadre of trained professionals with guns and badges. As she said often, "moral support is good, but muscle is muscle."

Armed with Becky's support, and her own sense of injustice, Kate knew she had political cover. With the support of her Advance team and the Secret Service, she knew she had operations and logistics covered in case Mr. X tried to mess with them during the veep's visit. For brief moments she felt like Mr. X had been neutralized.

While doing Advance, however, it's always important to remember that if everything seems to be going well, you should probably check your messages.

The gentleman who was in charge of West Virginia Democrats' day-to-day campaign activities, a man called Junior, was Mr. X's protégée, and he was to be her primary contact. Prior to her arrival he had dedicated considerable effort to envisioning the V.P.'s schedule from wheels-down to wheels-up in his head, without bothering to consult anyone on the V.P.'s staff. And he and had taken the trouble of committing it to paper, all four pages of it.

When Kate arrived in his office that afternoon, he handed her an official-looking document, titled, "Vice President Walter F. Mondale's Schedule."

"This is what we have in mind when the vice president arrives on Saturday," he told her. "We've run it by the powers that be, and it's been approved."

She asked him if he'd spoken with the vice president's scheduling office.

"Yes, I did, when they confirmed his visit, and we discussed this."

She knew he was pushing the boundaries of truth. Yes, someone in the Scheduling Office may have spoken with him to confirm the V.P.'s visit, and yes, Junior may have told that person, probably the Scheduling "desk," that he had suggestions to make about the schedule, but that was as far as any such conversation would have gone. The desk would have told him how much time had been allocated for the visit and confirmed the veep's participation in the rally. That's it. Then he would have been told to coordinate with the Advance team.

Junior's fantasy schedule was jam-packed with events, overloaded with expectation, blithely unaware of time constraints or even an acknowledgment that time passes when people move from one location to another. At first Kate thought she might ask if he'd invented a teleportation machine.

"Thanks so much, Junior," she said as she scanned his pages. "This is pretty ambitious. We only have two hours on the schedule for his visit, and the schedule I've been given by the VP's office calls for a rally and time for media interviews. I was under the impression that this is what was worked-out with Mr. X."

Junior didn't seem fazed. "That's not what Mr. X told me. We can do all of this in two hours."

"That may be true in a sense," she told him, "but it wouldn't leave time to get everyone off Air Force II, drive to any of the sites you propose, get everyone out of the motorcade and into the sites, move the traveling press into and out of each site, do individual media interviews, or drive back to the airport. All of that takes time. Each step is a long process. Each site requires production, press arrangements, electricity, security. I hope you understand that your proposed schedule is really too ambitious."

"Can't you get him to spend a little more time here and not run off so fast?"

"I'll certainly ask," she said. "Based on my experience, I'd say that the schedule will probably remain as it's been given to me, which calls for a rally followed by media interviews at a location that can accommodate both."

"Juss a rally and some fuckin' interviews? That's it? What the hell is going on here?" He was roostering-up, hackles flaring.

If he was trying to intimidate her, she wanted him to know it wouldn't work. She deadpanned, "I can't tell you what the hell is going on here, other than this was undoubtedly worked out between the White House and your boss. By definition that puts it above our pay grade. You should ask Mr. X that question."

"I will," he said. "Until then we should put this thing on hold until we work it out."

"Junior, I appreciate your advice, but I have three more days to produce this entire trip, so I need to be doing it now. I solicit any suggestions you have about a place we can do the rally, either indoors or outdoors, near an indoor location where we can do individual media interviews." By this point she didn't have a reason to trust any of his suggestions, but figured she'd ask to be polite.

"You juss keep in mind that we control the city. If you want to use a place, we have to approve it," Junior blustered.

"Duly noted, Junior. I'd like you to keep in mind that I'm just doing my job here. I've been sent to do a specific task and I have no position on this one way or the other. As far as I'm concerned you guys can trot the vice president all over town and hold him hostage for the remainder of the campaign. But my employer tells me what to do and they've told me to produce a rally. Until I hear differently from the White House, that's what I'm doing."

Junior's testosterone level may have dropped a point or two, but not enough to notice. "I understand," he said.

"Now, do you have any suggestions about a potential rally site?" she decided to ask bluntly. "You guys want this to look good as much as we do."

He recommended they look at a plaza between some government buildings downtown. It turned out to be the right choice.

As Kate had no illusions about the vice president's power to draw a large crowd, or lack of it, her first thought was to hold the rally indoors in a contained space. Within hours of her meeting with Junior, the Advance team identified three potential indoor venues which turned out to be unusable. The outdoor plaza Junior suggested had the elements they needed: a space that could be controlled visually (shrunk or expanded, as need dictated), dedicated motorcade access, good light, good access for press and public, indoor spaces for media interviews and holding rooms, and electricity. And it had a perfect spot for porta-potties. The weather forecast seemed fortuitous but game-day was four days away.

At Kate's request, Junior allowed the Advance team to use a small office in the state Democrats' campaign headquarters, which put them in close proximity to Junior and his staff. However, she also expanded the staff office in their hotel to allow space for the extra volunteers they needed. It also allowed the Advance team to work in an office for which they had the keys. Not that Kate didn't trust Junior; she was always a belt and suspenders kind of Advance woman.

West Virginia Democrats' state staff were great. They helped, to the extent their time allowed, provided resources and, importantly, sent volunteers. They understood that Vice President's Mondale's visit was also a good opportunity for them to organize, recruit more volunteers, identify voters and attract donors.

That lasted for a day. By Thursday morning, volunteers, and support in general, became an issue.

It was understandable. The visit of a president or vice president attracts a lot of interest. It's exciting. The people who are currently volunteering for the party or for individual candidates are the ones most likely to hear about the opportunity to volunteer for the Advance team—maybe get in on a little of the action, maybe meet the Big Guy.

Often, local campaign managers feel they're losing all their volunteers to the circus that came to town. Sometimes they get angry that the Advance team is stealing all their good people, 'cuz they are. Sorry.

The guy on Junior's team who was nominally in charge of volunteers, Marvin, at first was unconcerned about the Advance team and their needs. He wasn't obstructionist. He wasn't helpful either, but he didn't hinder their efforts. That was on Wednesday. In campaigns, however, light years can pass within a day, and by Thursday morning he was fuming at Kate over the phone.

"My staff can't function anymore because you've taken all of our volunteers over to your hotel to do whatever it is you have them doing," were the first words Marvin spat when he called at 7:45 a.m. Kate could hear the steam coming out of his ears. "We didn't bring you people into town to mess up our campaign."

"Marvin, we're going to have six people over here today. Are you telling me that's all the volunteers you have for headquarters?" she asked. "Seriously, they're great people, hugely talented and we appreciate them being here. But we didn't ransack your headquarters, did we?"

"We need those people here. We've got voter I.D. and a phone bank in progress," Marvin said.

"And I've got the vice president of the United States arriving on Air Force Two on Saturday morning at 11:30 a.m. to campaign for your bosses. Two hours later he'll be gone. Is this going to put a crimp in your campaign? What do you want me to do, Marvin? Are you asking me to handcuff the volunteers and physically bring them back to your headquarters? I mean, they asked if they could help."

Apparently, Junior had been listening on an extension. He spoke up unexpectedly. "No, just don't take any more. We're getting a lot of complaints," Junior said.

We're getting a lot of complaints? The last refuge of the meritless demand.

"Junior, here's the deal," Kate explained. "I'm going to need motorcade drivers, site volunteers and press volunteers to do this event, which means we're signing people up as we speak. Ya know? I promise they will all be returned by 2:00 p.m. on Saturday."

Junior shot back, "We didn't think you guys were going to fuck things up around here this much. We just can't give you everybody."

"How about I come over and meet with you and everyone who is complaining about this imposition and try to work out a compromise, because, I promise you, if this event ends up as a total failure, it *will* make national news. The reason you didn't expect to have to support the trip is because you've never been involved with a White House-level visit. This will be a good education for you." It was a snarky comment, but not quite as snarky as she would have liked. "So how about we meet and find a common ground?" She knew Junior wouldn't accept her offer of a meeting.

He demurred. "That's OK," he said. "I'll talk with Mr. X."

"Good, that will help," she said, even though she had absolutely no idea what that meant or how Mr. X could help, other than if Mr. X told Junior and Marvin to shut up and try to be helpful.

From what Kate gathered, either they didn't speak with Mr. X, or that's not what he told them to do.

By Thursday afternoon, one of the volunteers who was helping Nancy with her site arrangements informed her that Junior had given an order to his staff to stop helping the Advance team. It was the old circular firing squad for which Democrats are so famous.

The Advance team was still signing-up volunteers at that point, and most of their prime volunteer positions—motorcade drivers, press volunteers and crowd control/rally volunteers—were being filled. Given the task still before the team, and the uncertainty of their preparations, Kate thought it was a good time to call Mr. X for a little diplomacy. Junior's instructions to his staff bordered on sabotage.

Mr. X took her call; she thought he might not. It was her turn to be direct.

"Sir, I understand that Junior has told his staff to stop helping us. He's told them not let us have any more volunteers. At the moment, we don't have enough people to help us manage the event. It's kind of a 'basic' when you're putting on a major event with a Secret Service protectee."

"Can't you find some people who aren't already volunteering for us?" Mr. X asked. It was not an unreasonable question.

"We're certainly putting out the word beyond just your coordinated campaign," she told him. "But these people need to be vetted by us and name-checked by the Secret Service, and the Service requires at least 24 hours to do their security check." It never hurt to mention the needs of their Advance colleagues who represented federal law enforcement, whose needs are tangible and non-political. Usefully, often times the sound of their name—*Secret Service*—was intimidating for the locals. Kate had learned through experience that many of her local contacts believed the Secret Service had final approval of her schedule and political and production arrangements. They didn't.

Mr. X was undeterred. "Isn't that really your responsibility, to find volunteers? I'm being told that all of our reliable volunteers are now preoccupied with the vice president's visit. We just can't provide any more people."

"I completely understand, sir, and I'm sorry this has come as a surprise, but we are still filling volunteer slots." She felt compelled to brief Mr. X on the consequences of too few volunteers to help manage the events. "One example—we still don't have enough motorcade drivers, and if we are short of drivers we have to start eliminating cars from the motorcade. The first vehicle we will have to eliminate will be the VIP van, which law enforcement considers non-essential." (She invented that excuse on the fly, but it was true.) "That's the vehicle in which you're slated to ride when we leave the airport, and if you're not in the motorcade, there's a good chance you'll get stuck in traffic and miss the rally." The threat may have been a little un-subtle.

"I can get you a driver for the VIP car," Mr. X grumbled.

"That would be great. We'll need another driver in addition to that person, and probably another twenty volunteers for the rally on game day. Can you help with that? We will take good care of them; try to introduce them to the VP."

Mr. X was stuck. "I'll talk with Junior."

"Thank you, that would help immensely. I promise you, this is a good opportunity for your coordinated campaign. If we draw a few thousand bodies to a rally, your staff can use it to organize, hand-out volunteer cards, solicit small dollar donations. It can be a win-win." All of this was true.

For the second time, Mr. X managed to momentarily shock her. "I hadn't thought of that," he said.

"I realize that it seems we're sapping your resources, but there are a dozen ways you can use this visit to your advantage other than getting some media coverage and making sure that everyone who needs to get stroked gets stroked. I'll work with you to touch all the political bases you need to touch. You guys just need to tell us who you need to take care of, and we'll figure out how to accommodate them within the constraints of the schedule so it all makes sense logistically."

"Point well-taken, Kate," he said. "I'll talk with Junior again."

It was a breakthrough. She sensed that Mr. X's and Junior's worries were mostly about whose hands were going to be shaken by the VP and who would appear to be "in charge" as it was happening. Any staff member who had been sent by the White House to be the Lead Advance would have encountered at least some of the same jealous pushback. They were guarding their turf like a street gang because people are people, and testosterone is testosterone.

Kate's concerns centered on press coverage and the vice president's logistics, which were not incongruous with Mr. X's personal desires, unless Mr. X tried to drag the veep some place they hadn't planned.

The problem: Kate wasn't in a position to add another event, a receiving line essentially, that might eat twenty minutes or more. She had to integrate a combination of glad-handing at key moments along the VP's walking route, at the same time ensuring Mr. X's proximity during those moments, but not constantly.

When she arrived at the coordinated campaign office, Junior was still grudging but more accommodating. He was near the front door when she walked-in.

"So, ya big-footed me with Mr. X," Junior noted as they walked to his office.

"No, I didn't Junior. The White House did, and necessity did. It's in everyone's best interest that this visit turn-out well, and the fact of the matter is that if you guys just tell me what you want and who you need to take care of, I'll do my best to accomplish it."

It was apparent from the fantasy draft schedule Junior had created that his needs were not totally insurmountable. He wanted the veep to drop-in to a day care center; wanted the veep to go to a local TV station for an on-set interview; he wanted the veep to attend a VIP reception/photo receiving line prior to the rally. She had begun to integrate some of those desires into aspects of the rally site.

A little research into the day care center showed that it was actually a doggie day care, which Junior hadn't mentioned, and it was owned, coincidentally, by a major Democratic donor, and her husband was also listed as a major donor. They would have to be content with a brief handshake with the veep outside his holding room on the way to the rally. Once Kate had the veep securely placed in his holding room, she would task Mr. X with rounding up the "Doggie Day Care Donors" and positioning them just outside the Hold at the right moment.

Later, when Junior couldn't get his way, he continued to lobby hard for the vice president to go to the doggie day care. One of the volunteers told Kate that the woman who owned the facility was Junior's sister, and the real object was a photo of the veep in front of the building, which they could then use in their business promotion. That wasn't going to happen under any circumstance.

The TV interview that Junior envisioned as a "drop by" to the TV station would have to take place at the site, in the room chosen by Joe and Nancy. The VP would move from room to room for each TV interview that was requested, and Junior's favorite would get their own exclusive 4-minute interview just like all the rest.

Nancy designed the rally stage with enough room to accommodate a small number of bodies behind the vice president, with large additional space off to the side, almost out of the camera shot. Placement immediately behind the veep was reserved for local candidates for office, no more than a dozen. But Nancy and Kate could cram fifty local VIPs off to the side, blending into the "cutaway" camera shot, and they would still feel like they were in a place of honor. That space would have to suffice for the big-shots for whom Junior wanted a private reception.

Nancy, Brad and Kate did crowd-building for the rally, with Joe producing copious amounts of local press coverage about the event and its preparations. Nancy and Brad contacted every traditional Democrat-leaning organization in the state and in surrounding states, asking them to contact their membership. Kate arranged for senior citizen centers in the Charleston area with "active seniors" to send busloads of people, based on her promise to have special seating for them close to the stage. High school civics teachers were encouraged to talk about the upcoming rally with their students. Brad found a local marching band willing to play for a small fee.

The Advance team was a crowd-building machine. They didn't sit back and hope that people would attend, they actively pursued potential attendees, both en masse and individually. Much of their outreach was under the radar, retail-level. Mr. X and Junior were probably only vaguely aware of their efforts.

Junior's lack of "grasp" became starkly apparent when Nancy first contacted the contractor that he'd hired to provide staging, lighting, sound, seating, rope and stanchion for our rally. Given a budget of about a dollar ninety-five, the contractor was told by Junior to prepare for an event the size of a local PTA meeting. Junior essentially requested the equivalent of a Mr. Microphone and a boom box.

Nancy's first conversation with the contractor was an educational experience for both of them. The contractor, reasonably, didn't mind the thought of expanding the rally's production requirements and budget. Unreasonably, he neglected to mention that he didn't have most of the equipment she needed.

Early Wednesday morning, the moment Nancy informed Kate of the discrepancy in "expectations" for the rally, and the concomitant discrepancy in budgets, Kate called and left messages for both Mr. X and Junior.

It took the better part of the day to obtain Mr. X's reluctant agreement to fund the rally as it needed to be funded. It was a political, not official, event, and therefore had to be funded by the local party.

At the same time, Kate had already instructed Nancy to continue planning for the rally they'd envisioned, with the requisite amount of consideration given to press and security needs. There was no question that certain basic procedures had to be followed.

Mr. X had to qualify his budget acceptance with some sexist shade. "Our contractor tells me you've got some girl telling him what to do down there. You're not going to spend a bunch of that money on flowers and decorations and all sorts of girlie fru-fru's that we don't need, are you?" he said in his slight southern drawl.

She promised him they'd keep it "sparse and very masculine."

She didn't realize how sparse her production could become. It wasn't until late Thursday afternoon, the day before the "build," when Nancy pressed the contractor, Dave, for a delivery schedule. Dave informed Nancy he was having difficulty finding the staging, lighting and bleachers that had been requested. Nancy realized Dave had no ability to provide even basic sound equipment, such as a "mult box" for the press SO THEY COULD RECORD THE SPEECH. No mult box, no audio. If there's no audio, the only sound you'll hear on the evening news, IF they bother show to video of the speech, is the sound of the crowd making crowd noises over a faint voice in the distance. For radio news coverage it's a complete non-starter.

When Nancy asked Dave, the original contractor, if he had HMI's, a basic for lighting an outdoor production, he had no idea what she was talking about.

Nancy and Brad kicked-in to high gear to find other contractors, one at a time, that could provide equipment by the next day.

As a result, Dave "the contractor" called Junior "the fixer" on Thursday evening to inform him of the changes Nancy was planning and that she was bringing in other contractors. Dave was understandably worried about his income.

Happily, Kate had already informed Junior of their plans, but nonetheless he called her to "express his concern" on Thursday night.

Junior's drawl was thicker than Mr. X's, and Kate had to admit to a little bias with regard to southern accents, in that some are more pleasant than others. Junior's fell on the less pleasant side. This time, for some reason, it was more pronounced than before.

"Dave tole me tha y'all are stealing his show. Ya know he kinda needs the business and I promised him we'd use him," Junior said. "What the hell is goin' on with y'all?"

"Look, I told you about this. You tell him he'll make as much or more than he would have under your original contract because we will still need things from him, but he can't do the whole job. He doesn't have the equipment," Kate's voice rose, "he doesn't have the technical expertise," her voice rose a little more, "he doesn't have the ability to pull this off. Ya understand?" Her decibels were a distinct exclamation point. All of a sudden, she was talking to him like his mama. "Is this gonna be something you'll be proud of, or something you'll be looking for excuses for later?"

"I'll tell ole' Dave not t'worry about it," Junior drawled quietly.

She wasn't about to let up. "Please do. And please stop ringing me up every time somebody gets a burr under his saddle. Ya understand? I have to be able to do my job at this point."

"Ya know I'm getting pressure from higher up," Junior said. It was lame.

"From now on we're going to prioritize based on protocol," she told him. "That will make things easier. According to protocol order, the White House, the most senior officials in our country, are at the top. Vice President Mondale is going to walk in here expecting to see a real event, not a toddler's backyard birthday party. Let's get the basics of the White House's needs addressed and accomplished, THEN we'll deal with everyone else. Is that OK with you?" She felt good laying it out bluntly, although she didn't even lay out a tenth of it, excluding swear words and threats.

"That's OK," Junior said. "I'll try to leave you alone."

"Good, we understand one another. Thank you, Junior." Kate hung up, no goodbye.

Junior kept his word for a good two hours.

At 9:30 that night, Nancy was working at the Democrat headquarters after a meeting with her site volunteers. She was on the phone, still trying to find vendors, when Junior came back to the office with one of his staffers. They had been out to dinner and they'd been drinking.

"Hey there sugar tits," was Junior's greeting. "Why you workin' so late when you should be out havin' a good time?"

The young male staffer with Junior appeared surprised by the comment.

Nancy didn't seem the least surprised. She looked up at Junior. "I'm working here trying to fix what you fucked up. I see you're hard at work setting a proper example for your staff. Why don't you toddle your drunk ass out of here and let me do my work?"

"Uuuuuuu, she's getting belligerent," Junior slurred.

The young staffer tried to intervene. "Why don't we just let her do her job. She's obviously working."

Junior was having none of it. "Doin' her job fuckin' things up ya mean, bringin' in all her Washington friends to take over the whole thing. Juss you rememba this . . . we kin take over this whole thing any damn time we want. Say, is it true what they say about Washington women? They all juss as hot as you?"

Nancy looked at the young staffer, who looked embarrassed and helpless. She didn't try to respond. She gathered her papers and notebooks and belongings while Junior watched. She walked out of the office past him without speaking, and he reached out and grabbed her butt.

She spun around and hit him on the face with the back of her hand, which was holding papers. The sound of it was probably fiercer than the feeling of it, like hitting a dog on the nose with a rolled-up page of newsprint (which no one should ever do). It would have been difficult to determine who was more shocked—Nancy, who was grabbed; Junior, who was wacked upside the head; or Nancy again because she wacked him.

They stood looking at each other for a few seconds, Junior in stunned amazement, Nancy with angry determination. She continued to hold her ground.

"Wha' did I do?" Junior slurred again.

Nancy turned and walked out. When she arrived back at their hotel, Kate, Joe, Brad and Jill were in the staff office along with a few volunteers. Nancy asked Kate if they could talk privately; they went to Kate's room.

Hearing the news, Kate was livid. She immediately picked up the phone to call White House Signal and ask them to connect her with Becky, the director of Scheduling, but hung up before completing the call. She was unsure. Reporting the incident to the White House could, she feared, reinforce the "tricky" nature of sending females to do Advance. She felt they could be blamed in some way.

Nancy was less unsure. "Becky ought to know about this. What he did was beyond simple rudeness. It was an assault. And ultimately, he's trying to prevent us from doing our job."

"Totally agree. What he did was criminal, and you could file a complaint. And Junior will say he was just trying to be friendly and you misinterpreted," Kate said. "And he knows we're not likely to file a complaint because of the bad publicity it would cause."

"So what do we do about it? Let it slide?"

"We can't let it slide," Kate said. "But I'm not sure that going to Becky again is the wisest move. This would be the second time on this trip I've had to complain about male chauvinists."

"Male chauvinist assholes, you mean."

"She'll agree with us, but as it moves up the chain, I don't want anyone to start thinking that sending women to do Advance is more trouble than it's worth."

"How about calling Mr. X on him?"

"You think we'll get any understanding from Mr. 'women shouldn't do this job'? He'll brush it off," Kate said.

"This wasn't a matter of Junior merely acting inappropriately," Nancy said, "he grabbed me. I don't want to see that son of a bitch anywhere near this event."

"Nor I. Give me some time to think about it. Right now, I think I ought to tell T.J., and you should tell your site agent," Kate said. "Junior's comment about taking control of things raises it to another level, and that level of weirdness could definitely become an issue while the V.P. is here."

Nancy agreed. "Good point. Then at least we've gone on the record with law enforcement."

Once their volunteers left for the night, Kate and Nancy told the rest of the team and warned them to remain more vigilant than usual for any shenanigans on "game day." Kate was blunt. "I don't trust these guys any farther than I can throw them." Nancy was blunter. "And don't turn your backs on them, any of them. You guys neither. I can imagine what these West Virginia boys are capable of. You saw *Deliverance!*"

It lightened the mood.

Friday morning sparkled with radiant sunshine and new hope when Kate, Nancy, Joe, Brad and Jill met at 7:30 to coordinate their day. They decided work in their hotel Advance office and avoid the Democratic headquarters altogether.

Nancy and Brad spent the morning tracking down a contractor that could install the rally's sound system and coordinating volunteers who were putting leaflets out on the street. At noon, they needed to start coordinating their contractors' load-in's at the site.

Joe left at 1 p.m. to coordinate a poster painting party with twenty volunteers at the downtown community center, where he expected to garner local TV coverage of the rally preparations for the Friday evening news.

Kate and Jill stayed in the office, on the phone. Jill found the volunteer drivers she needed, along with one extra, at Kate's suggestion, "just in case." She acquired all their name-check information for the Secret Service, and finally received confirmation that the car rental agency would have the right cars for staff and press.

Prior to Nancy's departure, Kate took her aside to discuss Junior.

"Here's the best solution I can come up with. It's not like we'll be able ban Junior from the site. He's gonna want to be around, and he'll have Mr. X in his corner, and they know we won't make a scene in front of the vice president. So we put him in charge of the VIPs and keep the VIPs, and Junior, as far away from the V.P. as we can. We create an off-site meeting place for the VIPs, and Junior can escort them to their place on stage-left at the last minute."

"The VIP meeting place can't be too off-site," Nancy said, "or Junior will get wise. I've got a room we can use in another building. It's connected by a walkway; it's a short walk to the VIP area next to the stage."

"Perfect," Kate said. "Here's one more thing. I've found a caterer for the VIP room who will send the bill directly to Junior at the Democratic Party office. Order whatever you think the VIPs would like, except booze, and it will be a Monday morning surprise for our hosts."

"We should give Mr. X's VIPs the best that money can buy. Maybe a lobster and steak buffet," Nancy said, "or maybe a million-dollar plate of cold cuts. Whatever it is, I guarantee it will be expensive."

"What about pins?" Nancy asked. "You're not going to give any of them 'S' pins."

"Not a chance in hell," Kate replied.

("S" pins provide the wearer the highest level of access anywhere on-site, including to the "protectee" under the Secret Service system of identifying people who have been name-checked and cleared for security purposes. It's almost as good as a regular "staff" pin.)

Nancy continued, "Good. I was hoping you'd say that. Mr. X gets an "A" pin because we have to include him in the airport greeting and give him a ride in the motorcade to the site. Once he's on-site, he won't need access on his own. I prefer that we escort him anyway. What about Junior?"

"Junior? I'll still have the agents name-check him in the hopes of finding an outstanding warrant, but I'll do my best not to pin him at all. You or Brad will have to escort him as he's escorting the VIPs."

"I'll ask Brad to do that, for obvious reasons," Nancy said. "Plus, Junior hasn't met Brad yet. I might ask him to act like he's a Secret Service agent; Brad wearing a suit, wearing an earplug, talking into his hand, can pass for an agent, and Junior won't know the difference."

"Of course Brad can't actually say he's an agent," Kate cautioned. "But if Junior thinks he is, then tell Brad to do a body cavity search on the guy. Brad can tell him he's looking for drugs or hidden microphones."

"Nice touch," Nancy said.

"No, rough touch," Kate countered. "Rough and invasive."

"It's a nice fantasy," Nancy said. "I doubt Brad will share our enthusiasm for him looking up Junior's anal cavity."

"He's a former Hill staffer. He's used to having his nose up peoples' butts."

At 3 p.m. Kate and Jill dashed over to the site to look at the "build" as it was taking place. Kate also wanted Jill to familiarize herself with the entire layout because she would be leading the traveling staff from the motorcade to the staff holding room and doing other tasks as needed.

Joe arrived to oversee construction of staging for the press platforms.

The scene appeared chaotic to the uninitiated, specifically Mr. X and Junior, who had come to rubberneck. They spotted Kate immediately as she arrived and made the mistake of confronting her.

"Does she know what the hell she's doin'?" Mr. X asked, referring to Nancy.

Nancy was busy directing contractors and laborers in their work. It was organized bedlam.

"She knows EXACTLY what she's doing," Kate said. "She's done it dozens of times. How about you? I thought you and Junior were up to your eyeballs in organizing for the election? Why are you here?"

"We just stopped-in to take a look, see how things are goin'," Junior said.

"Uh-huh," Kate replied. "Thank you for your interest. Tell you what. I'm going to do a little walk-through with Jill. You gentlemen are welcome to look around, but please let Nancy do her job. She has enough on her plate."

She didn't wait for a response. "Let's go," she said as she motioned to Jill and they walked toward the press platform, where Joe awaited.

They paused for a few moments to talk. "See those guys over there?" Kate said. "That's Mr. X and Junior. Keep your eyes on them. Make sure they don't start messing with anything or anyone."

Joe had harsher words when he saw their nemesis. "Mr. X's head looks like a cue ball with fringe glued around the middle."

"Be kind," Kate said. "He didn't choose to look like a hairy carp, although he did choose that hair style. I'm certain he has personal issues that even he can't identify."

Kate and Jill then went to Nancy to inform her of Junior's arrival on-site in the company of Mr. X. Nancy was already aware.

"I saw them talking with Junior's friend, contractor Dave. I was keeping my distance," Nancy said. "I assume that's Mr. X with him. I could make a comment but I won't."

"That's probably wisest . . . " Kate started.

"On the other hand, I think I will," Nancy said. "Damn, that's the twerp who was acting like Mr. Macho man giving you grief. I could whip him and I'm a wimp. A fit wimp, but a wimp nonetheless."

"Hopefully it won't come to that," Kate said. "I asked them to leave you alone."

"That's what Junior's staffer asked him to do last night when he was drunk," Nancy pointed out. "Didn't work then . . . "

"Maybe Mr. X will chaperone him today," Kate said.

"I asked Brad to keep a low profile while they're here," Nancy said.

Kate acknowledged her point. "I understand."

As Kate and Jill continued their walk-through, Jill asked her why Brad had to keep a low profile.

"We may need him later," Kate explained, "in case Junior or Mr. X act up."

"Muscle?" Jill asked.

"More along the lines of moral intimidation," Kate said.

The final countdown meeting of the Advance team with Secret Service and White House Communications was held at the event site, in a small auditorium in the same building as the V.P.'s holding room and Joe's media interview rooms.

As always, Kate, as staff lead, and Special Agent Trapasso, as Secret Service lead, chaired the meeting. It was uneventful. There were no surprises and no concerns, because, as always, they were professionals.

Privately, immediately after the countdown meeting, T.J. asked Kate about the two guys who were hovering around the site earlier. "Were those your local political contacts?"

She confirmed their identities.

"They looked like they were up to no-good to me. They were really scoping out the place," T.J. said.

"That was my feeling, but then I'm biased at this point. I assume they're always up to no-good," Nancy said.

"Go with your gut. I will," T.J. said. The weather forecast that evening showed a slight chance of rain the next day.

Saturday morning the slight chance turned into a thunderstorm, but the forecast for rally time still looked good. Kate, Nancy, Joe and Brad were at the site at 7 a.m. making sure there was no damage to the equipment and staging that had been installed the night before.

Jill rounded-up her motorcade drivers at the appointed hour and began the process of collecting their cars and vans from the rental agency, after which they were to drive to Kanawha Airport in time to be "swept" by the Secret Service bomb team.

Back at the site, Kate and the team spotted Mr. X and Junior once again, at 7:45 a.m., poking around. Kate kept her distance; Nancy informed her site agent of their presence. It didn't matter much because everyone would be kicked-out of the site at 8:00 a.m. by the EOD team, Explosive Ordnance Disposal, for their final sweep. That might take a little less than an hour, at which time Nancy could open the gates for the general public.

At Kanawha Airport, Jill was gaining valuable new experience. She was finding out how seriously the Secret Service agent who was responsible for checking the backgrounds of those who are expected to be close to the vice president takes his or her job.

The job of doing name checks is rather tedious, and every agent has to take his or her turn doing it, but it sometimes yields interesting results. One of Jill's drivers found out the hard way.

A few minutes after the cars and vans arrived, as Jill was talking with her drivers, she was approached by her Secret Service counterpart, who requested a private conversation.

Special Agent White started with, "I have some bad news about one of your drivers."

"Which one?" Jill asked.

"It's a Mr. Messina. He has a warrant out for his arrest."

Jill, surprised, asked, "For what?"

"I can't tell you, but the police will need to have a private conversation with him down at the station," White said.

"You mean you have to take him away?"

"Yes m'am. A warrant is a warrant," White said. "What I don't understand is why a guy who must know there's been a warrant for his arrest would volunteer to drive, and give you all of his name check information."

"You have a point there. Seems pretty stupid to me," Jill said.

"How will that leave you for drivers?"

"Kate told me to name-check an extra person for just such an occasion, and that person is here to take Mr. Messina's place," Jill said. "I'll have her drive the straggler car."

"Which one is Messina? Can you point him out without being obvious?" White said.

"He's the tall guy with the reddish blond hair," Jill said. "The rubber-faced dude. Looks like all the Bowery Boys intermarried."

"Yes, I see him," Agent White said. "You're right, he looks like someone sat on his face. I kinda feel sorry for him. He doesn't know what's about to happen."

"He did it to himself. I'm guessing he won't be volunteering again any time soon," Jill said.

Agent White walked over to the group of volunteer drivers and, as Jill watched, he spoke with Messina then the two of them walked to one of the police cars that were parked nearby. Before he got into the police car, a local uniformed officer put handcuffs on him.

Jill still felt a little guilty because she thought he was sketchy from the moment she met him, but he'd come recommended by the local Democratic office.

After sending Messina off to jail, Agent White came back to brief the remaining motorcade drivers on their responsibilities during the motorcade, including specific instructions on how to drive and when and how to take bathroom breaks once they arrive at the rally site.

Kate arrived at the airport an hour before Air Force Two's wheels-down to be greeted by the news that one of their drivers had been carted-off by the gendarmes. She laughed, "Frankly I didn't see that one coming."

"You saw *something* coming," Jill said. "Whatever it was, we're lucky to have a back-up. I'll remember *that* lesson."

"Luck had nothing to do with it," Kate said. "You get burned once you don't forget the lesson. In my case, one of my drivers was too drunk from the night before to walk straight much less drive. Coincidentally, it happened in another southern city."

"What did you do?"

"I ended up having to drive one of the motorcade cars from the airport. For the next two movements I assigned my Site 2 from the first event. It worked out."

"What about Mr. X over there? Did you see him?" Jill asked. "He just drove up. Do you see who's with him?"

"Damn. Double damn," Kate said. "Junior's not supposed to be here. He's supposed to be at the rally site coordinating his group of VIPs. Looks like another confrontation on the way."

Kate walked the 50 yards to where Mr. X and Junior stood, chatting innocently. Junior was wearing a camera around his neck. When they spotted Kate, they greeted her as if they were old friends. It was creepy. They'd transformed into civil beings. Kate was her usual professional self, but she was having none of it.

"Junior, I thought you were hosting your VIPs at the rally site. What are you doing here?" Kate asked.

Mr X spoke up. "Our photographer couldn't make it, so I asked Junior to come take pictures when we greet Vice President Mondale. I didn't think you'd mind."

"That's fine by me," Kate said, "but he'll have to find his own way back to the site. We don't have room for him in the motorcade."

"He has his own transportation. He'll be OK," Mr. X said.

"And what about your VIPs? Who's minding them now? Is Nancy aware?" Kate asked.

"They've all been told where to go," Junior said. "Jim from our office staff is with them."

Kate smelled a rat. Junior was wearing some dinky camera around his neck, not very convincingly.

Junior asked about one of the motorcade drivers. "Where's Messina?"

"Why do you ask?" Kate asked.

"He asked if he could be one of the drivers, so I submitted his name," Junior said.

Like a frame in a cartoon strip, a light bulb went off over Kate's head. Messina was Junior's guy.

She politely informed Junior of Messina's unexpected detour. "Apparently he was needed elsewhere," she explained, "so he left."

"He left?" was Junior's surprised reaction. "Where?" He seemed a bit too excited.

Kate was beginning to smell an even rattier rat. "Dunno. You'll have to ask him." She walked away leaving Junior stunned.

Special Agent Trapasso pigeon-holed Kate shortly after she walked away. Aware of the trickiness of Kate's situation, he seemed almost sheepish when he informed her that he'd have to put a pin on Junior.

"We can't have that guy walking around here with no pin. None of the other agents know who he is. I'll give him a "G" pin, (the lowest level of access), just so they know he's been name-checked."

"Can you give him a pin that instructs the Secret Service to shoot him on-sight?" she asked. "Like a big red X?"

"We stopped using those pins after the Nixon administration," he told her.

"Damn, finally, one thing that I agree with Nixon about. It would certainly make life a lot easier sometimes," she said.

"Not for the guy we shot," Trapasso said. "And the liberals wouldn't like it."

Kate wasn't comfortable with Junior being there in the first place. Having the legitimacy of a Secret Service-provided pin on his lapel heightened her sense that misdeeds were afoot. When Air Force II arrived, she kept a close watch on him.

Air Force II pulled-up to its arrival point and Kate escorted the group of five greeters to the base of the staircase as it extended down to the ground. When the flight crew opened the door, Kate went up into the plane to brief the vice president. She was greeted by Becky and they both went into the VP's cabin.

Vice President Mondale greeted Kate warmly. He liked Kate, as did everyone. "Becky tells me they've been giving you a tough time here. How did it go?"

"We worked it out sir," Kate assured him. "I paid some guys to beat up a couple of guys, and they've been very cooperative ever since. You know how it is."

Mondale laughed. "Is that what they call hardball politics?" he asked.

"In this part of the country it's called effective communications," Kate said.

"Well, let's hope they didn't hurt anyone too badly," Mondale said.

"We provided some wheel chairs so they could attend the rally," Kate said.

"Very thoughtful of you," he replied as he chuckled.

Kate gave Mondale his briefing cards for the first two movements, handed copies of all the cards to Jim Johnson, the administrative assistant, then exited the plane and down the stairs followed closely by the V.P.

Sure enough, when the vice president came down the stairs he was greeted by the expected greeters—the mayor and his wife, Mr. X who wasn't married and probably never dated, and the local county clerk and her husband —plus one. After clicking photos of the receiving line with his Brownie camera, Junior jumped in at the end to become a greeter and handed the camera to Mr. X. Mr. X looked as if he expected the last-second maneuver.

It didn't come as a surprise to Kate. She thought it wouldn't be the last of Junior's shenanigans.

Junior started to try to say something to the vice president and Kate stepped between them. She aimed her comments to all the greeters. "Thank you, everyone. Please remain here until the motorcade has pulled away. Thank you, Mr. Vice President."

Mondale stepped away quickly and got into his limo as Kate stepped back and spoke at Junior. "Really Junior? All that effort to scam a handshake with the vice president?" She looked back at him with disdain as she walked to the police car at the head of the motorcade. When she reached the door, just before sliding into the back seat, she looked back at the motorcade to see that everyone was in place and ready to go.

Once the motorcade departed, with T.J. and Kate in the back seat of the "Lead Marked Car," Kate heard the ear plug on her walkie-talkie come to life.

"Kate, Kate, this is Jill. Over."

It took her a moment to reach the radio and turn up the volume, then she spoke into the microphone that dangled into her hand from the wire that traveled up her sleeve. The equipment was a heavy pain in the ass, but in this case, it came in handy.

"Yes, Jill, I can hear you. Over."

"Kate, it looks to me that we have an extra passenger in the motorcade. I think Junior jumped into the Staff van just as we pulled away. Over."

"He what?"

"Looked to me like Junior jumped into the Staff van as we were pulling away. Over." Jill repeated.

"Thanks Jill. We'll talk when we get to the site." Kate didn't want to extend the conversation on a walkie talkie that could be heard by anyone with a scanner.

She turned to T.J. to inform him, "Now we know why Junior tried to get his felon-friend to be one of our motorcade drivers. He intended to jump into the motorcade. I have to say, Junior has just stepped over the line. He got into the Staff van as we were pulling away. Obviously he isn't manifested. There wasn't space for him in the van, so I don't know how he's crammed-in. He just lost his event rights as far as I'm concerned."

"Absolutely agree," T.J. said.

"As soon as we get the vice president in the holding room," she told him, "I intend to find him and take his pin. If he wants to participate as part of the general public, he'll have to go around and go through the general public's entrance like everyone else. But we can't trust him anywhere near the vice president."

The motorcade pulled up to the site and disgorged its occupants. As the traveling press was escorted to the press area, Kate led the VP to his holding room then went hunting for Junior. Along the way she gathered Brad, who looked very official in his dark suit, white shirt, dark tie, and ear plug. She pulled her '76 campaign "hard pin" from her pocket and handed it to him. It was a non-descript design in gold with yellow cloisonne. "Wear this," she said.

Junior wasn't hard to find. He was in the room that Nancy reserved for the VIPs to gather. The room was just outside the innermost security perimeter, but still inside the backstage area.

Kate summoned Junior to the hallway, where Brad stood waiting and looking quite serious. He didn't introduce himself to Junior.

"You decided to become part of the vice presidential motorcade. What am I supposed to think about that?" she asked.

"I didn't think you'd mind," Junior said, glancing occasionally at Brad. "There was an empty seat."

"No, there wasn't an empty seat, and there is no empty seat in this event. You're outta here. Give me your pin," she demanded.

Junior hesitated, as if he might not give it to her. He glanced at Brad again. Brad glowered back at him.

"What?" Kate said. "You're lucky I don't throw your ass in jail. You can go have a nice visit with your friend Messina. Yeah, that's where Messina is at this very moment, cooling his heels. They arrested him, and HE didn't even do anything. You, on the other hand, did. Hand over the pin."

Junior started to say something and Brad cut him off with a simple, "Sir."

Junior slowly reached up to his lapel and removed the tin pin. Brad held out his hand and Junior gave it to him.

Brad then said, "Come with me."

Brad than walked behind Junior out of the building, down the sidewalk past the motorcade, then up to the rope line that delineated where the public space began. There was a small opening forming a gate that was guarded by a uniformed police officer, through which Junior was forced to walk.

"Sir," Brad told him, "If you want to watch from the public area you'll have to walk around and go through the magnetometers." Brad then turned to the police officer and said, "He's not to be allowed back in here." Brad didn't wait to see if there was any response from the officer.

Back at the VP's holding room, Kate, Nancy, Brad and Joe converged one last time before the rally. Kate and Brad regaled their colleagues with their story of triumph over Junior and Junior's walk of shame. Between fits of laughter, Kate warned them not become complacent. "Just because Junior is on the other side of the rope line doesn't mean nothing else can go wrong. Don't get cocky."

Brad then went back to the VIP hold and escorted the group to their side-stage vantage point. Once Joe confirmed that the press was in place, Kate told the vice president they were ready.

The rally was a real rally. Nancy and Brad pulled-off a beautiful event despite the obstacles. The crowd was estimated at over 4,000 (which equates to 8,000 in Advance parlance). The vice president's speech was enthusiastically received, the local candidates were happy because they'd been given a chance to speak, prior to the vice president's arrival, to the largest audience they'd ever encountered, and the press had a great story to cover.

After hand-shaking his way off stage, the vice president stopped at one point to shake a few more hands . . . the hands of Mr. X's top V.I.P.s. Nancy set them along Mondale's walking path back to his holding room. The brief greetings went smoothly because Mr. X wasn't there. He was still on stage with his other VIPs, caught up in the post-event revelry.

By that point there were only two items left on the schedule: a brief handshake with the Democratic donors, with Mr. X in attendance, then three five-minute interviews with the local television stations and one with the Charleston Gazette and the Daily Mail together.

Nancy found Mr. X and his big donors, the doggie day care owners -- Junior's sister and her husband -- and placed them near the vice president's holding room for the promised quick handshake. Kate briefed the veep about the grip.

As Kate was escorting Mondale out of Hold, en route to the media interview rooms and surrounded by a small group of Secret Service agents, Brad walked up to whisper in her ear. "The entire VIP group from the stage is just outside the curtain down the hall to our right." It was the security perimeter, guarded by agents standing "post" and blocked by a pipe and drape. He told her, "Mr. X said he'd bring the vice president down to visit with them."

Kate stood back and looked at Brad in quiet amazement. "That isn't gonna happen," she whispered back.

She stopped at the group of three, Mr. X and his guests, and stood next to Mr. X, smiling. The veep stopped to do his duty. They'd brought a camera so Brad was drafted into service as a photographer. Two clicks for safety.

As the second click went off, Kate said "Thank you, Mr. Vice President" and began to lead him away.

At that moment Mr. X stepped forward and said, "Mr. Vice President, I've got fifty of my biggest donors down that hallway waiting to say hello to you. Could you spare one minute?"

Mondale looked at Kate. Kate looked at Mr. X and said, "We really wish we could, but the schedule is extremely tight. You should have mentioned this a few days ago when I arrived. We have some media interviews that we have to get to at this very minute."

Mr. X implored the vice president. "Just one minute?"

Mondale looked at Kate then back at Mr. X. "I'm going to follow my Lead Advance. She sounds like she knows what she's doing."

She smiled at Mr. X and motioned to Brad to join her as they walked to the first interview room. After a short distance she told him, "Escort Mr. X and his guests out past the pipe and drape and get his security pin. I don't want him coming back in here."

Brad put on his best Secret Service look-alike face and sound-alike voice and did just that. When he spoke to Mr. X he said simply, "We need that pin back now, sir." Mr. X complied without a whimper. Once outside the pipe and drape, he was neutralized.

When the veep went into the first interview room, Brad cornered Kate. He handed her something from his coat pocket and told her to stash it.

Kate looked down and saw the little point-and-shoot camera that Junior was using at the airport. "Where'd you get this?"

"Junior left it in the VIP room when you kicked him out of the event. One of the guests told me whose it was. I told her we'd return it to him."

"Which we will, in perfect working order," Kate said. "You didn't make any promises about the film inside, did you?"

"No m'am," Brad said. "Only the camera."

"Junior was using this at the airport to get shots of the greeters, including Mr. X and the little slime ball himself. You know, if he'd just waited an hour, he'd have gotten all the shots of himself and the vice president that he wanted. I told him we'd have him there with his sister and brother-in-law. What an idiot."

"The place seems to have more than its share of interesting personalities," Brad said.

"You're kind. I'm out of kindness. I'll take the film and get it developed, then send the mayor and the county clerk their photos and misplace Mr. X's and Junior's. I can be pretty mean for a minister's daughter."

"Sounds like poetic justice to me," Brad said. "I'm glad you're not going to ask me to pray for their souls or something. After I've left town and a few years have passed, then I'll forgive them."

"Good plan. After you've forgiven them, I'll send them their photos," Kate said, "if I can still find their address."

The remainder of the trip passed smoothly. Kate finally relaxed during the motorcade ride back to the airport. Agent Trapasso told her that Mr. X had caused a commotion outside the pipe and drape, attempting to get back in to see the vice president. Apparently, Mr. X experienced the futility of arguing with an agent standing post and was not very happy about it.

Both Kate and Agent Trapasso found that hugely amusing.

At the airport, after the vice president thanked the motorcade drivers and Jill, his motorcade Advance person, he took a moment to thank Kate.

"You did a great job on this trip," he told her. "It was a great rally. I assume that bald guy we took pictures with at the end was the one who gave you so much trouble?"

"Yes, sir. But frankly I think they would have been difficult for anyone to deal with."

"Thank you for all your hard work on this," he said as he walked up the stairs to the plane. It was all she needed to hear.

Jim Johnson followed the vice president and echoed his sentiments before rushing up the stairs. "Thank you, Kate. Great job. See you next time."

Finally, Becky spoke to Kate before getting back on the plane. "Sorry for all the bullshit you had to endure. I promise we'll send you someplace nicer next time."

There was always a next time. Next time might be the best time she ever had on an Advance trip. As for this time, she was about to make it a good time.

Kate and Jill left the airport after calling-in wheels-up to the White House, and found Nancy, Brad, and Joe as they were finishing breaking-down the site.

The team decided not to wait for their airline flights, which were scheduled for the next day, to exit town. They would take two of the rental cars and drive back to DC. It was worth the six- or seven-hour drive, although the first few minutes of seeing Charleston in the rearview mirror would be the most satisfying.

After returning to their hotel, packing their bags and their cars, Kate had one more errand to run. She decided to return Junior's camera personally with the help of the Advance team. Nancy was given the honor of the formal presentation.

They drove together to the local headquarters, each in jeans and t-shirts for the road trip, and parked in front. Kate could see through the storefront window that they'd hit the jackpot. Mr. X was there as well.

The team— Kate, Joe, Nancy, Brad and Jill— walked in together, smiling. Mr. X and Junior appeared surprised, maybe even taken aback.

"We just came to say thanks for everything," Kate said.

Mr. X, looking at Brad, said "I thought that guy was a Secret Service agent."

"I never said that," Brad said.

"We never said that," Kate said.

Brad added, "And did you really think that Secret Service agents take tourist photos of people in a greeting line? Did you think that I was with the Secret Service P.R. department?"

Nancy walked up to Junior. "Hi, pencil dick. Here's your camera." She smiled politely, handed it to him and pivoted to walk away.

Junior examined the camera immediately. "Where's the film?"

"Dunno," she said as she walked. "That's how it was given to me."

"But where's all my photos?" he implored.

"Tell you what," Kate said, "when I get back to DC, I'll go to the White House Photographer's office and see if they have any shots of you guys with the vice president. If they do, I'll try my best to get them for you. The only problem, as you know, girls aren't very competent when it comes to things like that."

With that they all smiled politely and said a quiet "thanks." Nancy said, "See ya next time," and they walked out of the headquarters.

Kate called me in the VP's Advance office on Monday to tell me the story of the trip.

"Jacques," I heard a familiar voice say.

"Simmons. How was your trip?" I asked.

Advance people are always eager to swap war stories, especially the horrific ones. It worked. I was horrified. She asked me to clear her into the Old Executive Office Building on Wednesday so she could go to the Photographer's Office to look at proof sheets from the trip.

She stopped in to see me that day to report the results of her search. One proof sheet contained all the pictures of the VP's arrival as well as those of his handshake with Junior's sister.

Kate told me she asked the young secretary who ran the office, "How can I make sure some of these photos never see the light of day?"

She told me the secretary glanced through them and shrugged, "These are just some handshakes, right?"

"Yes," Kate said.

"We still have the negatives," the secretary told her, and promptly handed the sheet to Kate. "You want it?"

Kate said "Yep" and took 'em. She told me she ordered copies of photos with the big donors and other unsuspecting innocents and would send them to the right people. Then she would take home the contact sheet and file it for future reference, meaning that any remaining physical evidence of Vice President Mondale shaking hands with bad people on the trip would forever dwell in the deepest, darkest labyrinths of the national archives, unknown and unseen by anyone.

I told her it seemed like small recompence for the trouble she'd experienced.

Kate told me it was worth the effort. "You do what you can do. Mr. X and Junior will go nuts trying to find photos of themselves and their family members with the vice president, while everyone else who was involved will have received their own. It will drive those guys crazy. Maybe they'll think twice the next time they have to deal with female Advance staff."

I promised her that Mr. X and Junior would forever be on my personal shit list if I ever worked in West Virginia again, which didn't happen for another twenty years. By that time those gentlemen were no longer around. Kate, in her long political career, never returned to the state to do an Advance trip.

CHAPTER 4

Detroit, Labor Day 2008, Obama, the Democratic Nominee for President:
The Greatest Event in Presidential Campaign History (that didn't happen)

It was supposed to be historic and fantastic. It was supposed to be the biggest event of the campaign and the holy grail of my advance career. I was supposed to create iconic visuals that would rank among the most memorable in American presidential politics. It was supposed to be Barack Obama's 2008 Labor Day speech in Detroit in front of over 110,000 wildly enthusiastic people.

When Obama headquarters asked me to do the Labor Day event, they mentioned they had given the event a title: the "Detroit Rally for America's Workers." It was a hugely symbolic speech for an important national audience.

Two of my political heroes, President Harry Truman and then-Senator John Kennedy, gave historic Labor Day speeches in Detroit in the memorably named Cadillac Square. Both were campaign speeches, Truman in 1948 and Kennedy in 1960, when they were the Democratic nominees. Ever since my first presidential campaign in

1976 I'd wanted to advance Labor Day in Detroit for the Democratic nominee for President of the United States.

Within the space of a few days that summer, my hope of fulfilling a career-long dream soared to extreme heights only to find it like Icarus, cast down and drowned in a sea of reality. Multiple realities, really, all of which were outside my realm of influence. There can be few disappointments greater in the world of presidential politics than watching helplessly as the potential for a massive, meaningful, poignant event disintegrates due to mere logistics. OK, mere logistics, and bad weather—but not even the weather in Detroit but the weather a thousand miles away—and a massive downer of a speech. Nothing even close had ever happened to me before.

Initially beside myself with giddy anticipation, there I was, in Detroit, in late summer, tasked with creating a rally at the end of the Labor Day parade for the very popular Democratic nominee for President of the United States, Barack Obama. Sadly, things were about to get mediocre.

The beauty of Cadillac Square (as I perceived without having advanced it) was that it could hold more than 100,000 people. Press photos from '48 and '60 showed the crowd beautifully, and I knew that I could create even more stunning visuals with 21st-century technology and the Advance techniques we'd developed since the days of Truman and Kennedy.

Based on my previous year's experience as Obama's lead Advance, there was absolutely no doubt in my mind that he would attract a crowd larger than 100,000. It was easy to conjure—the largest crowd of the entire campaign—as if it was happening before my eyes. I was already planning to rent forklifts for camera positions and enough bleachers to seat 20,000 people around the perimeter.

Prior to arriving in Detroit on the morning of August 29 for the fast three-day advance, I was informed by headquarters that the speech should take place at a pre-selected location. The scheduling "desk" told me there was a jazz and food festival taking place on the riverfront, Hart Plaza, where there would be a stage already constructed. Obama headquarters thought we could use that stage. As a result, our production costs would shrink considerably, as would the Advance team's budget.

There was no point in arguing, but none of *that* was going to happen as far as I was concerned. I would be forced to waste time looking at the Plaza and providing headquarters with a reasonable excuse why it was inappropriate for our purposes, but Hart Plaza wasn't going to happen. Someone didn't get the memo that only place to hold a Labor Day speech in Detroit is Cadillac Square.

Upon arrival, I quickly gathered the team's Site 1, Jamie Ax; Press 1, Jan Allan; and Crowd Advance person Pamela Turlington and alerted my Secret Service counterparts who always arrive in town before the Advance team. We raced to Cadillac Square for what I was certain would be our first "walk-through" of the site I had definitely chosen for the speech. The Square was located at the end of the Labor Day parade route, where tens of thousands of people would converge naturally, so it was perfect in both size and proximity to the greatest number of warm bodies.

All I needed to do was determine where the main stage and the press risers would be placed, and we could work out the logistics from there.

The Secret Service was waiting when we arrived. A half-dozen agents were gathered in a group on a traffic island on the edge of the Square, looking up and around, and appearing quite concerned. The instant I stepped out of the car I knew my dream had flown out the window. Thousands of windows.

Cadillac Square had changed since 1960 and it sucked, to put it mildly, as an event site. The topography didn't work—it sloped away in strange places and provided no natural spot for staging, either for the main stage or the press platforms—and was completely surrounded by high-rise office buildings, mostly vacant, with more windows than could be counted, let alone secured.

Each one of those windows was a potential "hide" for a sniper, and there was no way in the world that Secret Service anti-sniper teams could cover all of them. There was also no possible way for the Service to search all those buildings, with all of those offices, and secure them from someone entering later.

Agents hate that, but I'm not an agent. Those things aren't really my problem. My mission is about political communication, while their mission is security. On the other hand, I understand that it's impossible to have a campaign without a candidate, so I try to be understanding of the Service's needs. My decision was made easier by the fact that, even absent all of those high-rise buildings, the site still sucked as a place to hold a speech. Did I mention it sucked?

As I walked toward the agents, they looked at me, apparently expecting the worst. Less than an hour earlier I told my counterpart, Special Agent Jim White, that Cadillac Square was going to be the event site. They expected to have to talk me out of it. Their faces were grim.

"Don't even worry about it," were the first words out of my mouth, even before the introductions. "I'm sorry for having dragged you out here, but I thought it would save us all time. Obviously, the site isn't great from your perspective, and it doesn't work for us either. By the way, I'm Steven Jacques, the Lead." I then introduced my team members and each of the agents introduced themselves.

Special Agent White expressed his relief. "I thought you were going to tell us we had no choice, that you were going to use this site no matter what."

I told him, "If we'd all had an extra day to fart around with this, I might have taken two or three minutes to lead you on and let you believe we were coming here no matter what. But we don't have time for even a couple minutes of a practical joke at this point. I've got to find another site. Any suggestions?"

When appropriate, such as when I was desperate as hell, I liked asking the agents from the local field office if they could recommend a possible site. In this case they had none, except to suggest that we bring Senator Obama to the local Secret Service field office and let him do the event from there. I wasn't quite that understanding of their security needs.

Promising to call Special Agent White the moment I found another site, the team and I were off to search the downtown area, or anywhere near the downtown area, for a place that would hold a bajillion people. It was freaking Labor Day, in freaking Detroit, and we were going to create the biggest event in presidential campaign history. Dammit.

We immediately went to Hart Plaza on the riverfront, which was lovely and might have held 30,000 people if it weren't for a large food and jazz festival that clogged the site and the sight-lines. In addition to a crappy little stage that did nothing more, for our purposes, than take up valuable space, the site included dozens of food tents, trucks, and truckloads of equipment crowding the area. Seems they had a permit or something.

Once we saw the riverfront site it was clear I didn't have to lie about it. It wasn't a good site. It was disjointed and shrunk to such an extent that it could hold five or six thousand people, maybe.

The team split up. We checked-out every park, ball field, high school track, motel parking lot, vacant lot and bocci-ball court anywhere near somewhere that might be considered sort of downtown-ish. We wanted to make it as easy as possible for the tens of thousands of people who attended the parade to find their way to our event.

The Advance gods never smiled on us. After a few hours of frantic searching, we were forced into submission. It was like someone died. I was forced to choose Hart Plaza.

There were at least a hundred thousand people out there waiting to be given a place to stand and watch and cheer for Barack Obama, and I was about to tell ninety-five thousand of them "Sorry, we have no room for you." The small size of the site guaranteed that many, many would stand in line for hours, in the heat, inching toward the magnetometers to get in, only to be told that the site was full.

That's the kind of lifelong memory for which I do not want to be responsible.

Almost as tragically, I was forced to set aside my own fantasy. In my imagination I already had a poster-sized blow-up photo of the soon-never-to-happen 2008 Labor Day event—taken over Obama's shoulder as he addresses the unbelievably massive crowd splayed-out in front of him—framed and hung behind my desk at home. I was even going to ask Obama to sign it, which, as an old-school Advance man, I eschewed. And I was going to ask him to sign it big.

My hopes and dreams and home décor notwithstanding, I had no choice. It would be the riverfront site in the midst of all the food tents and supply trucks. With all that *crap* clogging the place.

Jamie, Jan, Pamela, and I put on our game faces and approached the site as we would any other. If we were given lemons, we'd make lemonade, as we always do. The question was how to make the site work for our purposes. What were the best visual angles to capture the excitement and enthusiasm of the moment? Where could we take the telegenic shot that would convey the candidate's leadership, his connection to organized labor and to the needs of everyday working women and men?

Nowhere.

There was only one place we could put the main stage and only one place we could put the press riser, which meant we had no choice for a backdrop. It was a long narrow space with some shrubbery and odd concrete structures around it. And there was no way to make it look like anything else. We'd throw up a typical banner and some typical bunting and it would look nice. Festive. Typical.

Directly behind the narrow space was a wall, and we couldn't move away from it. As a result, there was no room to put much of anything behind the speaker's podium, and it took all our effort to squeeze a ten foot "buffer zone" in front of the podium for the Secret Service.

There were no easy cutaway shots, no overhead angles, maybe a couple of cute little up-the-nose close-up angles, and a sizeable chunk of the audience's view had to be blocked by the press riser.

Jamie, as Site 1, was tasked with building the site. It wasn't what he'd hoped for because he too was a student of history, but mostly he wasn't fond of shoe-horning an entire rally into a pea-size labyrinth.

But hell, it was Labor Day in Detroit. The day and the city still had cachet. Jamie had already set about finding the contractors and equipment and labor to build it all before close of business.

Coincidentally, Labor Day, ergo the Labor Day Parade, happens at the end of what's known as Labor Day weekend, when members of most labor unions don't work. Who knew? We found out how hard it is to find union labor in a union town on Labor Day weekend, even for a pro-union Democratic presidential nominee. It seems that many of those folks would rather enjoy the three-day weekend they had been planning for weeks rather than help us make history. There is no accounting for some people's priorities.

The "build" was to be on Sunday evening and all night, which meant paying lots of overtime. We thought that would help . . . our contribution to the local economy.

We decided to make the speech site feel like a community event. Instead of an iconic, solo presentation, we would pack the stage with Detroit's labor and community leaders. If the event couldn't be huge, we would make it intimate and warm. If Obama couldn't speak to the masses, we would surround him with them. Sort of. That would be our visual.

Another word for that is "clusterf**k," but I was confident we could manage it. Jamie and I had worked together many times through two presidential campaigns, and we had experience making the moving pieces of large events work in tandem, or fixing events that had begun to teeter on the edge chaos. This time we knew what to expect because we were creating it.

DAY 2 - Saturday

The team went to the site early to finalize our design, and it took more than the usual amount of creativity and time to feel as if it would work. Placement of the main stage, press risers, sound and light equipment, crowd movement and control measures, given the bizarre layout of our site, came down to discussions of inches.

As is often the case when creating a large event in limited space, tension arose between "Press" and "Crowd" Advance over the size of the press riser and the extent to which it blocked the view of our crowd.

Jan's (Press I) concern was the news media's access to the site and their visuals, including the best possible view of the speaker's podium and easy movement to the "cutaway" (a secondary side view of the stage).

The news media take up a lot of space, and those who travel with the candidate (the traveling press) become irritable when they're provided with less than the usual accommodations. It's in our best interest to make it easy for them to cover the story. A few were known to get downright mean when they didn't get what they wanted. (No names)

Paula (Crowd Advance) was rightfully concerned that some of the audience wouldn't be able to see Obama as he was giving his speech. Her mission on this Advance trip was definitely not traditional "crowd building." Her challenge, which was considerable, was "crowd management," including the care and comfort of those who were lucky enough to get in.

There is no doubt in the minds of most Advance professionals that our real audience at an event is the news media in attendance. Crowd Advance staffers sometimes disagree, but the reality is that the general public is in many ways a useful prop. How the crowd looks on TV, especially how large and enthusiastic it looks, is part of the Advance team's special mission.

That's not to say that every individual in the crowd isn't important. The audience reaction to the candidate will have an impact on the news media's perception of the event and the candidate's popularity locally. We want every audience member to be happily enthusiastic during the event and happily enthusiastic afterward, just in case she or he runs into a member of the press who asks, "How did you like Obama's speech?"

Jan and Paula each had their valid arguments, which could ultimately be resolved only when the "build" (construction of the site) was underway on Sunday night. The placement of Jan's press platform limited not just the view, but also Paula's and her volunteers' ability to move the audience into the event.

Nothing about the site was going to be easy.

Aretha Franklin

After the "Detroit Rally for Americas Workers," Obama was scheduled to attend a picnic with plumbers and pipefitters in Monroe, south of Detroit, which I was tasked with creating with another Advance team. I headed there by mid-morning.

Along the way my trip brightened considerably when headquarters called to inform me that Aretha Franklin wanted to attend the

Detroit rally. They gave me her cell phone number and asked me to contact her directly to make arrangements.

That doesn't happen every day. Even if you've been doing presidential advance for a hundred years, you don't often get a chance to meet Aretha Franklin and you don't get her personal cell phone number to coordinate with her directly. The opportunity to hang out with Ms. Franklin almost made-up for losing the best event of my life. *And she would have liked being part of an historic hundred-thousand-person event!* (Forgive me, I'm obviously still upset.)

I called her immediately, despite the fact that I had no specific information to provide regarding her arrival time, arrival place, escort, or holding room. She was warm and understanding and I promised to get back with her as soon as I could verify all the times and movements. I gave her my name and contact information, which became a lovely moment when she told me she liked my name and thought I should pronounce it in the French way. When I told her the only way I'd do that was if I became an interior decorator, she laughed.

Saturday became a day of pleading with headquarters for more budget. Despite the fact that we plopped our event in the middle of another on-going event, and there was "stuff" (staging, production equipment) on-site that potentially could have been of use to us, none of it was. Quite the contrary. We were required to build an entire event from nothing and wedge it between the equipment already there.

Jamie also managed to talk headquarters into increasing our budget enough to include a jumbotron closed-circuit monitor to place just outside our tiny site, in front of the Memorial to Joe Louis (the giant fist sculpture), where he would stream video of Obama's speech… to enable some of the *freaking 95,000 people who couldn't get in* to watch remotely.

The odd spaces and angles, and creative placement of buildings, roads, and parking garages around our site would make the logistics of moving our crowd a nightmare. Placement of the magnetometers through which our crowd had to pass became a negotiation with the Secret Service, who found it equally difficult to figure out.

My team settled-in for a "normal," average, run-of-the mill, challenging-as-hell Advance for an abysmally average presidential campaign rally. The remaining day and a half before we started to build the site was filled with the normal sprint to make it as good as we could.

DAY 3 – Sunday

The afternoon was marked by my second opportunity to talk with Aretha Franklin. Once we'd designed the site and decided where and when VIPs, including the heads of the Teamsters and United Auto Workers unions, would need to arrive, I called.

She didn't answer and I was crestfallen. I left a voice mail.

A few minutes later my phone rang, and I recognized the number as hers. She was gracious and interested in the details, and I told her how exited all of us were that she was attending.

As far as I was concerned, her participation was easily the best part of the entire event, and I told her so. "I was expecting a crowd of over a hundred thousand people would come to see Senator Obama, and I think they would have come, don't you?"

She agreed. "Yes, yes. In Detroit? Certainly, that many people would show up to see him."

I told her my tale of woe and she was sympathetic. She also expressed her confidence that it would still be a nice event.

I had every confidence that it would look O.K., maybe more than O.K., on television. The site would be packed with people, which alone is a formula for success even if the site only holds five or six thousand. It's better to have a small site that is packed with five thousand people than to have a large site that is half-empty with fifty thousand people. In Advance, there is no such thing as "half full." If only half the site is filled, it's half-empty. If a site is 90% filled, it's still half-empty.

We had to wait until the food and jazz festival shut down for night before we could begin our build. Contractors delivering equipment were scheduled down to the minute, which never works, as were the stagehands and laborers we'd hired. They didn't work very spectacularly either.

Much of the labor required to set-up press risers, staging, and barricades fell to the stagehands' supervisors and Jamie, who was injured at 3 a.m. when a heavy piece of staging landed on his leg as they were constructing the press riser. Despite the injury, he continued to work through the entire night.

DAY 4 – Monday, Game Day

Monday morning dawned hot and sunny in Detroit. In Louisiana—yes, Louisiana—they were bracing for Hurricane Gustav's landfall later in the day. Obama campaign headquarters told to me the schedule might change as a result, but my events in Detroit and Monroe would be unaffected. So I was led to believe.

As always, I met Obama's plane at the airport and drove in with my Secret Service counterpart in the lead marked car in the motorcade.

When we arrived at the site in late morning the scene was set. The crowd, most of whom had been waiting and snaking through down-town Detroit for hours in line, had filled the space. Local press was set, and the traveling press made it easily to the designated area. Our VIPs, including Aretha Franklin, were in their places. Teamsters President James Hoffa and United Auto Workers President Ron Gettlefinger gave rousing remarks about Obama's support of orga-nized labor, and they promised union support for him in return.

The audience was enthusiastic and primed to hear a barn-burner from the man of the hour.

It wasn't to be.

Obama was introduced and when he began to speak, he sounded pretty upbeat. He started by acknowledging Aretha Franklin, singing "Chain, chain, chain . . . chain chain chay-een." The man is no Sam Cooke, but the crowd loved it.

He praised labor unions and their lasting contributions to our county's prosperity, and then switched focus. The energy level sank to a low I've never seen at a political event. It was as if he tied a cou-ple of cement blocks to the rally and threw it in the Detroit River.

Obama spoke of the expected devastation that was about to befall New Orleans once again at the hands of a hurricane, which was ap-propriate at that moment when national concern was running high, given the devastation wrought by Hurricane Katrina in 2005. Media attention was focused on the region, expecting the worst.

He then announced that he wasn't going to give a speech. *That* caught my attention. Then he asked for a moment of silence for the people on the Gulf Coast who were taking shelter in preparation for Gustav.

It took a while for the crowd to calm, but it did mostly. Apparently, the sound quality was poor in areas of the site that were tucked around corners and behind food trucks.

When he began again, it sounded as if he was making a rhetorical transition from his concern for potential victims of the hurricane to broader policy concerns. He used the storm as a metaphor for the serious problems facing society as a whole.

Given Obama's facility with language, I expected him to deftly maneuver toward a compelling, maybe even electrifying message. Nope. He's a man who views caution as a virtue and he absolutely, positively did not want to sound as if he was giving a rousing speech, or anything that sounded like a campaign speech, when masses of people were about to be suffering.

He asked the crowd to also remember those who are suffering from "quiet storms" such as unemployment and underfunded schools, and then it was over. He didn't lie . . . he hadn't given a speech. His remarks lasted about ten minutes and were the exact opposite of a speech. It was more of a dirge. I don't think I was the only one in attendance who expected something more uplifting.

It so happened that I was making my way over to Ms. Franklin just before Obama asked for the moment of silence. Once that was finished, I again attempted to slide toward her without causing a stir.

Then Obama stopped speaking. I did a double take at him that would have made a mime proud, then over at Ms. Franklin, who had a look of surprise, then back over at Obama as he stepped away from the podium and started shaking hands along the rope line. I never did get to meet Aretha Franklin.

After appropriate thank-yous and good-byes, we, Obama, the motorcade, traveling staff and press, Secret Service, and cops were off to Monroe for a barbecue.

My Secret Service counterpart, Jim, asked me in the car what I thought of the event. My response was, "Was that an event?"

In my never-ending quest to see the silver lining, no matter how depressing, demoralizing, upsetting, and scarring a situation may be, I finally seized upon a perspective in which fortune smiled on us on that Advance trip.

My only solace, it occurred to me, was that Obama would have given that exact same non-speech if a hundred thousand people HAD been there to see it. If a hundred thousand hopeful and enthusiastic people had witnessed it, had waited in line for hours to participate, had been rockin' to the music we pumped through the sound system for two hours, had felt the energy level rise as the masses eagerly anticipated his arrival, it would have been a bummer beyond description. I believe that a hundred thousand people would have left Cadillac Square looking for a puppy to kick. Dejected, upset that they'd bothered, their desire to go to the polls diminished, Obama would have lost votes. Hell, he might have lost my vote.

As it turned out, media coverage of the event was decent. At least one media outlet reported that twenty thousand people attended. The visuals, both on TV and still photos, were up to standards. A few people were quoted as having been disappointed, but no one dwelled on it. There were reports that sixty-thousand people stood outside the rally watching it on our jumbotron.

No one and no media outlet I saw mentioned a comparison to historic Labor Day speeches of the past.

Just like what I now call "The 2008 Detroit Downer for America's Still-Unsung Workers," Hurricane Gustav was a non-event. Thankfully it wasn't nearly as severe as Katrina, nor did it hit New Orleans.

I never used Aretha Franklin's cell phone number again, but it lives in my day planner, forever remembered but unrequited, as will my fantasy of a history-making Labor Day event to catapult my candidate into the White House.

And I can say with absolute confidence that if the Detroit rally had turned-out as I envisioned, I would have taken credit for Obama's victory.

The next week I was in Red Bank, New Jersey, having a lovely time hanging out at the home of Jon Bon Jovi, advancing a fundraising event. This made Detroit easier to forget, despite the fact that Jon Bon Jovi is, disappointingly, a paragon of virtue who lives the life of a happily married civic leader, so my sex, drugs and rock and roll fantasy fell by the wayside too. Two fantasies destroyed in two weeks. Advance is hard.

CHAPTER 5

Poker, a Prescript to Chapter 4, Disappointment In Vegas

Rewind a couple of months from Labor Day back to June 24, 2008, in Las Vegas, Nevada, to the second most disappointing day of my Obama campaign experience. Ironically, it was preceded by an evening of one of the best times I had during the campaign.

To be fair, I started with the Obama campaign a week before he announced his candidacy in 2007 and there were only two times during the twenty-two-month campaign where I felt this way. Both times were blows to my professional creativity and had no measurable negative impact on the campaign as a whole.

On the other hand, there is absolutely no doubt in the minds of all those who agree with me that Obama would have won the election by a much larger margin had my creative license been allowed full expression. But how do you measure things that didn't happen? What is the opportunity cost of unrequited genius?

It was the juxtaposition of high expectations and low reality—seeing my brilliant ideas, which would have made both Detroit and Las Vegas iconic moments in presidential campaign history, dashed into nothingness— that made the trips so deflatingly similar.

Vegas

Despite the fact that I kept asking not to be sent to Las Vegas, the campaign kept doing it. Maybe it was *because* I kept asking not to go there. And when they did send me, I asked them to house me, along with my advance team, in a hotel *not* on the Vegas Strip. There was a nice Hampton Inn, north of the Strip, that suited our needs perfectly on a couple of trips.

Try doing an advance while staying in a hotel on the Strip. You have to walk twenty minutes (through the casino, of course) to get to your car in the parking garage, traffic in and out is a bitch, and almost all the events are in the suburbs. You can't park in front of your hotel, run in for something, then run out again to your next meeting. All advance operations are made more difficult AND there are no coffee makers in the rooms—coffee costs seven dollars in a coffee shop if you can find one, breakfast costs a hundred bucks, there are few television stations available on your room TV, and staying on the Strip means total immersion with crowds of people who are in Las Vegas by choice, which I cannot comprehend.

The advance team arrived on June 18 and was billeted at Caesar's Palace, on the Strip, once again, despite my entreaties. Why? Because Obama was scheduled to RON (remain overnight) there on June 23, prior to our events the following day, and the advance team had to stay there as well. It's one of the reasons I wasn't fond of doing advance trips that included RONs.

I was tasked with creating a town hall meeting at the most unexpected and beautiful location in Las Vegas, Springs Preserve, a

180-acre nature preserve, botanical garden, and state museum. Obama headquarters wanted an event focusing on green jobs and they pre-selected this site. This time I was pleased with their choice.

It's one of the reasons why advance is fun; often the unexpected is absolutely delightful. My main job site for a few days was a stunning state park, in Las Vegas, which is not known for its natural beauty, unless you include the Mother Nature Casino and Hot Wax Emporium.

But we still had to navigate the inconvenient environs of Caesar's, including a lot of walking. The journey to and from the garage alone was epic, but resulted in a valuable discovery. On day two of my forced-meanderings, I noticed construction taking place on one side of Caesar's, and it looked like a concert production, but simpler. The people supervising the work didn't look like roadies. They looked like producers.

I couldn't help myself. I approached one young lady with a clip board and asked about the staging.

The woman was indeed a producer and she couldn't have been nicer. "We're with *The View*, and we're going live from here all next week."

It was a classic 'light bulb went off in my brain' moment. I confirmed, "*The View*, with Barbara Walters?"

She confirmed it. In a nanosecond I hatched a plan. Three things popped into my head almost simultaneously.

First, within the previous couple of months I had seen Barbara Walters on one of the late-night talk shows describing a time, recently, when she saw Obama at a party. She said, "I told him, 'You should be on our show some time.' And Barack said, 'I *was* on your show.'

And I said, 'I wish I'd been there.' And he said, 'You *were* there.'" She admitted that she'd forgotten.

Second, Michelle Obama had just appeared on *The View* within the past few weeks. She was a hit, of course.

Third, I thought of Dean Martin, or Bob Hope, or Sammy Davis, Jr., doing a "walk-on" on *The Tonight Show with Johnny Carson*. It was classic. Best yet, Obama could do it and it get away with it.

Then a fourth thought occurred to me. "What would he say once he got out there?" One doesn't simply walk out on stage in front of people and stand there with nothing to say. I thought of this line, "Hi, I just came to introduce myself to Barbara Walters. I'm Michelle Obama's husband; my name's Barack."

It was inspired. It was a rare opportunity. It was the summer of '08, we'd wrapped-up the nomination but not the election, and it seemed to me that *The View's* audience was probably very similar in demographics to the Obama campaign's target audience.

And it was fun, and it would take Obama a total of five minutes to garner millions of dollars' worth of positive press, not to mention the tacit endorsements of the ladies on *The View* when they greeted him warmly. For my part, it was a bit of a set-up because I knew that the hosts of the show *would* greet him warmly. It was natural.

The context and rationale for a walk-on was solid, so I introduced myself to the producer, told her why I was in town, and mentioned my idea. She loved it. I added several caveats, the most important of which were that it was unlikely to happen and that she shouldn't tell anyone of the possibility. I did not want to establish any expectations beyond a faint hope.

It's been my experience that people who work in the headquarters of Democratic presidential campaigns aren't fond of creative ideas emanating from the road, which is another reason why advance is fun. Sometimes I do what I want and don't tell anyone at headquarters, which was easier before there were cell phones. It's my job as lead advance to garner positive press for the candidate and there are times when I can identify opportunities "on the ground" that staff working remotely cannot appreciate. It's always worked out well or I wouldn't have been asked back.

The producer gave me her contact information, and the game was on. My first step was to talk with my Secret Service counterpart, Special Agent Don Harris, to discuss the possibility of an OTR (off-the-record movement) and the logistics of doing so.

As expected, the logistical aspect— moving Obama from his suite to the TV production set— would not be easy. It required a long walk, as always, snaking through the casino in public view. There were no service corridors or adjacent elevators through which we could move unnoticed.

Special Agent Harris wasn't all that happy about the possibility of walking his protectee in public view for several hundred feet, but he was helpful nonetheless. I had done such movements before and seen them work. The element of surprise is key, as is the speed of the movement. Obama, surrounded by his little crowd of agents with the lead agent and me in the lead, moving at a quick pace with serious intent, was enough to leave any would-be glad-handers or evil-doers flat-footed.

I wasn't worried that such a movement might offend some of the onlookers whom we would blow past. On the contrary, most people's reaction to seeing such commotion is enthusiastic interest. They'll call their friends and tell them, "Guess who I just saw." Also, I would have been hard-pressed to believe that the voters in our target demographic were in a casino at eight o'clock in the morning playing black jack. Or the slots. I had no data at the time to back that up.

I remained in contact with the show's producer over the weekend to let her know that I was still working on it, re-confirming her desire and ability help make it happen at the last minute, repeating my note of caution that there was, in my estimation, less than a 50-50 chance of it actually happening.

She asked what my cut-off time was, and I told her if we weren't there within fifteen minutes of the start of the show, we weren't coming. Privately, I thought I'd be able to pull it off, but I hadn't decided when to ask Obama if he'd do it.

Monday Night

Since the start of the advance, Obama's draft schedule called for him to arrive at McCarran Airport at 5:30 p.m. on Monday, June 23, with our public events starting the next morning. I gave no thought to the fact that there was nothing on his schedule for that evening. I figured they would fill it eventually. My concerns were focused on Tuesday, both the scheduled events and the hoped-for unscheduled OTR.

That blank part of the schedule remained unchanged and I paid no attention. Obama arrived on time, we drove to the hotel (try parking a motorcade next to Caesar's Palace), Obama settled into his suite, and Reggie Love, his body guy, asked one of my motorcade drivers to take him out to look for playing cards and poker chips. Once again, I paid no attention.

Marvin Nicholson, Obama's trip director, and Robert Gibbs, the press secretary, came downstairs to meet me for dinner, and as we talked, Marvin said something about playing poker later and mentioned something about me joining them.

Marvin had a reputation for enjoying gambling a lot, as well as a reputation for losing. I, on the other hand, was fairly well-known in the campaign for being a stick-in-the-mud, primarily because every advance team I'd worked with had witnessed it.

I demurred at first, telling him, "You know I'm not a big poker player, and I'm not fond of losing money, so . . . "

Marvin then spoke more clearly. "None of us are great poker players. Come on, it will be fun."

I continued to baulk. "It's not really my thing."

Finally, Marvin said bluntly, "You don't understand. We're playing poker later in the boss's suite and he wanted to know if you'd like to join us.

That made it clear. My reaction: "Oh in that case yes."

He told me to meet at the suite at seven o'clock. *That's* what was on, or not on, Obama's schedule for Monday night. He was in Las Vegas and he enjoyed playing poker, but only where it was legal. That old Obama caution.

It's not like I'd played poker often in my life, but since the first time, in high school, when I was given a cigar by one of the other players and I won some money, I always made it a point to have a cigar when I played. Not necessarily to smoke, just to have as a talisman. Plus, I go all "George Burns" when I have a cigar.

I went rushing through the hotel and the lengthy mall attached to it with minutes to spare and found no cigars. Unbelievable. It really put me off my game. I went into the suite feeling at a disadvantage.

Joining our little group, in addition to Obama, Marvin, Robert, Reggie and me, was Arun Chaudary, the campaign videographer. We sat around a long rectangular table with Reggie and me at the far ends. We each chipped-in sixty dollars (thanking goodness that I was carrying sixty dollars) and Reggie handed out chips in varying colors, signifying sixty bucks in value.

The dealer named the game as the deal rotated around the table. While the rest of us opted for the well-known games, such as Stud or Texas Hold'em, Obama knew a dozen variations on poker (with complicated rules) that none of us had ever heard of, the names of which I will never remember.

I finally asked him where he learned all the poker games. His response, "Springfield."

The reference eluded me. "What's in Springfield?"

"The state capitol," he said.

I felt like an idiot. It wasn't that I'd forgotten he'd spent twelve years as a state senator, it's that I never think of Springfield, Illinois, except in terms of the Lincoln home.

My only response, "You spent all that free time in Springfield playing cards and you didn't go out an enjoy the vibrant social scene?"

He said, "What social scene?"

"Exactly," I grumbled. "You have no idea what you missed. I would have been partying with the glitterati."

As the oldest and stodgiest person sitting at the table, that line got a laugh.

At one point in the light banter someone made an obscure reference to Franklin Roosevelt, which reminded me of a story that I shared with my new poker buddies.

"I read that FDR, early in his administration, would sometimes play poker with his favorite members of the press corps, and when he lost, he'd pay his debts with checks. The thing was, no one ever cashed his checks."

Obama, who was sitting to my left, looked up, turned to me and smiled.

"So, get your checks printed as soon as you move in," I said.

There was no other response from anyone at the table. I guessed there was an unwritten rule that no one spoke of what happens after you win. That old Obama caution.

Later in the evening, as my pot of chips was growing from my occasional winning hands, I decided to mention *The View*. "You know, coincidently, *The View* is shooting live in front of Caesars' tomorrow morning, just as we're leaving for our first event. It would be a perfect opportunity to say hello, do a little walk-on." I thought it would spark some conversation. I was wrong.

Crickets.

I tried to continue. "It would take all of five minutes. I've worked it out with Service." Not being an extra pain in the ass to the Secret Service was a selling point.

Again, silence. I surmised that this conversation, which to me was all about the fun of creating positive media coverage out of nothing, was considered "business" by the folks at the table. Apparently, there was an unwritten rule about not talking "business" while playing poker. As far as I was concerned, being creative *was* the fun part. It's my idea of having a good time on a trip.

I shut up about it and restricted my comments to more appropriate topics, such as whether you can wear button-down shirts with suits. (I was "pro," Reggie was "con.")

It was a memorable evening nonetheless. They were all good company. We played until past 1 a.m. and I doubled my money. Marvin was the big loser; Obama broke even or came out a little ahead.

When we broke for the night, Obama surprised me by asking about *The View*. He'd been listening.

"So what's the deal on *The View* tomorrow?"

I explained the Barbara Walters set-up and rationale for him doing an unscheduled walk-on, and suggested the line that I'd thought of - "I just came to introduce myself to Ms. Walters . . . "

Obama said, "Well, it's a good line, but let me think about it."

To my unsophisticated ear, that sounded like he told me he was going to think about it. I just love it when I'm precious like that.

June 24, Game Day

Obama was scheduled to depart his suite at 7 a.m. to go downstairs to the exercise room and I made it a point to be there when he walked out.

When he saw me outside his door his reaction was simply, "What."

I didn't waste his time. "*The View*. The walk-on. Millions of viewers. Tons of media coverage later."

His response, "I thought we nixed that."

I stifled my first reaction. I said, "No, we didn't nix that. You said you'd think about it."

"Let me think about it," he said as he left with his Secret Service gaggle.

It finally occurred to me that "let me think about it" might mean no, but I was undeterred.

I immediately went down the hall to Robert Gibbs' room to beg him to make a pitch to the boss. Robert agreed with me and he sounded sincere, so I asked him to go down to the exercise room to convince our candidate. It was that kind of campaign; people were willing to talk.

While Gibbs' made the pilgrimage I waited in his room. It didn't take him long to come back and report.

"He won't do it," Gibbs said. "He says he feels that he'd be stepping on Michelle."

There was no point arguing, but I did anyway. "She was on the show weeks ago. Opportunities like this don't come around every day."

"I know I know. But he won't do it." He threw up his hands. There was no doubt he'd been down that road before.

That old Obama caution, or humility, or reticence, once again reared its conservative, risk-averse head. I was miffed, but showing my own "Obama humility," I kept my mouth shut. And kept on keeping it shut.

As we embarked on the day's scheduled activities I maintained my distance from Obama, which certainly isn't strange because at that point my duty is to lead him, not chat with him unless there's a need. I made sure there was no need. He wasn't going to get lost if I wasn't there to tell him where we were going.

He apparently noticed, because later that morning as he was walking past me to enter the town hall event at Preserve Springs, and I was facing away from him, he patted me on the shoulder and said, "It's ok," and kept going.

I said quietly to his back as he walked away, "If we lose, it was because of *this*." I emphasized "this."

He turned slightly toward me and smiled a little. I guessed he was thinking, "Whaddya mean 'we'?"

In hindsight, it may have been an augury.

The entire incident was upsetting, but not nearly as horrible as finding out, on my next trip five days later in Independence, Missouri, that Obama doesn't like barbeque. At least Kansas City barbeque. And this man wanted to be president?! You could have knocked me over with a feather. What kind of person . . . ? I had arranged a varied barbecue feast for lunch in the holding room of the Truman Auditorium where we held the rally. He had his choice: Ribs, pulled pork, chicken, beef, all the sides.

After spending twenty minutes out in the Auditorium rally site I meandered back into the holding room, anxious to find out if Obama enjoyed his barbeque feast.

His reaction? "It was a good rib."

I was shocked. "That's all you ate? A rib? Did you even try the sauce?"

Obama looked at Reggie and asked, "Where's the sauce?"

Reggie pushed a container of sauce across the table. Obama stuck the tines of a fork about a nanometer into the container, pulled it out and touched it too his tongue.

"Good sauce," he said.

It was beyond shocking. The following words fell out of my mouth: "Are you some kind of communist?" I don't remember his reaction.

I must live with the fact that I didn't tell the public before the election.

Both Las Vegas and Independence had their own happy endings in their own ways. I made sixty bucks playing poker in the former, and I took home a couple racks of ribs in my briefcase in the latter. I told Obama "I'm not leaving them for you Visigoths." Wrapped 'em up and stuck 'em in. Giant ribs. Ate on those suckers for days.

And of course, everyone knows that Obama lost the election and eventually faded into oblivion. So, lessons learned.

CHAPTER 6

Three Weekends with Bernie

My brief interlude as a Sanders advance staffer involved a total of three Advance trips, with three rallies, over the span of three weeks beginning on February 21, 2016, ending abruptly at 7:30 p.m. in Springfield, Missouri, on Saturday, March 12.

Just thirty-six hours prior to that moment in March, I was leading an advance team that had been scrambling to produce a rally in Columbia, Missouri, in a venue that I had just locked-in that morning after a frantic twelve-hour search. The venue, a livestock arena on the campus of the University of Missouri which could hold three thousand people, was the only available venue in all of Columbia. We found it at 1 a.m. Friday. At 4 p.m. Friday, and after a short night and long day of preparations, we were informed by Sanders' headquarters that the trip had been cancelled and the rally moved to Springfield, but was still scheduled for the same time as the one in Columbia, (doors open at 4 p.m. Saturday; rally at 7 p.m.). We then had twenty hours to produce a rally in a new town in an unknown venue.

For the first time in the forty-year span of my Advance career I had been sent to a city, (Columbia), where the entire city could ultimately not pass "vet," or clearance. Not just the one venue—the whole city was an inappropriate place to hold a rally. So said Bernie.

Once Senator Sanders was informed that Columbia was on his schedule *for the next day*, he decided it was too politically danger-ous because of previous racial tension on the campus of M.U. He feared becoming embroiled in a racially charged moment similar to one he had experienced in Seattle the prior summer with the Black Lives Matter movement, which has nothing to do with the campus organization at M.U. His decision to quit Columbia was based on inadequate knowledge of the campus organization called One Nine Five Zero (1950) and their mission, but no one bothered to ask his "eyes and ears on the ground"— his Advance team.

Background

Horror stories about Bernie Sanders' scheduling operation had been circulating for months before I finally accepted a trip. In the loose-knit community of Democrat Advance operatives, the slapdash na-ture of Sanders' personal involvement in the schedule, and its domi-no effect on his campaign, was well known very early.

The Advance operation was responsible for making the schedule work despite his best efforts to make their missions impossible.

The director of Advance, a talented young attorney named Marc Levitt, my colleague and friend from the Obama campaign in '08, had been in contact with me about doing Advance for Bernie begin-ning with his announcement rally in Burlington, Vermont. At that time, I declined Marc's kind offer for several reasons, not the least of which was that I felt Sanders couldn't win the nomination.

Sanders' prospects were dim in my view based on two simple facts: (1) the Clinton campaign and Secretary Clinton herself were years ahead in organizing and experience, and (2) Bernie's manner; he's too easy to caricature as one-dimensional. It has been well-documented that far too many voters base their decision primarily on emotion— "How do I feel about that person?"— and I wasn't willing to subject myself to the long hours of hard work, angst and worry, which in my case are unavoidable when doing an Advance, on a quixotic adventure, or at least not for someone else's quixotic adventure.

The campaign schedule was ruled, according to reports, with little or no regard for the Advance preparations necessary to create setpieces, most often rallies. As a result, Sanders' Advance teams were often tasked with producing large events on extremely short notice, often less than twenty-four hours and often on weekends.

Hair-raising tales of Sanders' mercurial management were too numerous and specific to be a figment of Advance staffers' vaunted imaginations, where every challenge, crowd and success can take on mythic proportions. The worst of the stories involved an Advance team of two people being sent to a small town in the Northeast at 8 p.m. on a Saturday with instructions to produce a rally the next day at 7 a.m.

Imagine, if you will, trying to locate all the necessary local people, along with their personal phone numbers, on a Saturday night. Try finding a venue and the people who run it, or try even asking around for local input about where to find a venue, or a space, or the equipment, to produce a large rally the very next day. If you do find the right people, see if they're willing to jump out of their weekend easy chairs and work their butts off for the next twelve hours, and beyond, to make your candidate look good on television for a night.

As time passed and the campaign progressed, I heard from Sanders' Advance staff and others that Bernie didn't understand the role of "Advance" and didn't respect it or the people who perform it. He was fond of asking, "Why can't we have our field staff put these events together; why do we have to hire all these extra people just to do Advance?" That attitude is usually a deal-killer for me.

However, one of the fun parts about doing Advance is finding out what presidential candidates are like in the Holding Room, out of public view. As a voter, I too would like to know how candidates act in private. I want to know how the candidate handles stress, and just as telling, what qualifies as stressful in his or her mind? Curiosity alone makes it difficult to turn down an opportunity to do a presidential campaign Advance trip for a Democratic candidate I've never met.

Forgotten in these preparations, at the most senior levels of the campaign, was the fact that teams of people—Staff Advance, Secret Service Advance, production companies, local police, local campaign organizers— must mobilize, plan, and coordinate all their efforts, jamming two- or three-days' worth of work into hours. Often, each responsible team has to make do with the "stuff" they have or what they can get with limited options. For the Staff Advance, this in-volves acquiring everything from an appropriate venue to produc-tion equipment such as staging, lighting, audio, risers, bleachers, pipe and drape, metal barricade, as well as event volunteers, who have to be trained.

Very often, and most aggravating for the Lead Advance, short lead-time involves shortages of magnetometers—which are provided by the Secret Service and are a fact of life for any Secret Service protectee. Magnetometers, or mags, are those little gateways through which you must pass to get on an airplane or attend a presidential campaign event. They are the choke point between the waiting crowd and an empty arena.

Secret Service agents have claimed since the invention of the "mag" that they can screen four hundred people per hour through each one. As much as I respect the Secret Service, which is a lot, that's a complete fiction. If people were naked and running, they couldn't put four hundred people per hour through each one. The number is closer to two hundred to two hundred and fifty, and therein usually lies the rub, at least for the past four decades of my Advance career. The mags always create a massive bottleneck, but they are run by people with guns and badges, so Staff Advance (civilians) have no control over their operation.

This simple fact, this constraint, has been the bane of my existence on "game days" for as long as I can remember. There has been, and always will be, this mathematical disconnect between Staff and Secret Service. Service *never* brings enough mags, unless the "principal" is the President of United States. Then they have plenty of mags.

For presidential candidates, there may be thousands of people lined-up in a half-mile long queue but they will only be allowed to enter as fast as the screeners can screen.

The Secret Service usually utilize their own uniformed division officers to staff the mags, and they are usually the most efficient. However, when their resources are stretched, Service uses TSA screeners from the local airport. Believe me, these individuals are every bit as efficient screening people for a presidential campaign event as they are at the airport.

All screeners, no matter who, are also at the mercy of factors beyond their control, including the amount of gear that the general public brings with them to the event. Despite the Advance team's media advisories stressing the need to leave bags, backpacks, and purses at home, the public does what it wants. And in winter months it probably would seem a little crass to ask people to not wear heavy coats and layers of clothing, especially when they might have to stand outside for hours waiting to get in.

However, the flow of the crowd is primarily limited by the number of magnetometers that are available, and the number of mags available is directly related to (1) the total number of mags the Secret Service owns nationally, and the availability of staff to run them, (2) the amount of lead time that the Service has been given to plan and ship, and (3) the number of protectees, probably other candidates, who are holding events at the same moment. The Secret Service simply does not own enough magnetometers to provide a large number— say, ten— for each candidate for every one of their events every day "just in case."

It's impossible to overstate the amount of stress that presidential campaign seasons, with multiple candidates, place on Secret Service resources, personnel, budgets and time. When an individual presidential candidate regularly puts unnecessary additional hurdles in the Service's path, such as routinely scheduling major events on short notice, it stresses their capacity, and probably patience, further. (One wouldn't know, however. They're very stoic.)

All of the aforementioned is to say that among the thousands of things that the Staff Advance team can and must control to produce a successful, nationally televised presidential campaign event, the mags ain't one 'em. My only strategy to compensate for this mathematical disconnect is to choose an outdoor site and then claim that a gazillion people are expected to attend, hoping this will cause Service to bring more mags. It seldom works.

On game day of my third, and last, Bernie Sanders Advance trip we had three "walk-through" mags and three hand-held mags that were used solely to rescreen those who had set off alarms on the walk-though's, to accommodate a crowd of seven thousand. At seven hundred and fifty people per hour, that works out to approximately way too long for people to get in the building, and it was somewhat self-inflicted by "the Sanders campaign" itself.

By "the Sanders campaign," I'm referring to Sen. Sanders.

It Begins

In early February, Marc emailed again and I agreed to help if Sanders came to Kansas City. By then I was appreciating Sanders' message about economic inequality and income disparity, and I assumed that doing an Advance for him would be a one-time gig.

On the afternoon of February 20, a Saturday, Marc called. Bernie, he said, would be in the Kansas City area, either Missouri or Kansas, on Wednesday, February 24, for a 1 p.m. rally.

That meant starting the Advance on Sunday, which meant I wouldn't have a venue until at least Monday afternoon. That meant we couldn't announce it to the public until then, or tell the Secret Service so they could begin their site preparations, or figure out exactly what equipment was needed until then . . . for a rally with "doors open" at 10 a.m. Wednesday.

I should have said no, but I had given my word and there's a little too much Frank Burns in me. Major Burns, from MASH, famously said his "wife trapped him into marrying her." "How?" he was asked. "She said she liked me," was his answer.

Well, Marc kept calling. One trip, I thought, and that would be it. I'd get to dip my toe into the presidential race for a few days, make my own assessment of the candidate and his campaign, then return to my normal life. That's the beautiful thing about Advance.

The First Advance

My Advance team wandered into town over the next two days. It drove me nuts. I predicted failure in my mind a thousand times on Sunday and Monday as I searched for the right venue and waited for my team and wondered how the hell we were going to pull it off. Assuming the worst, I hadn't expected much in the way of professionalism or experience from the Sanders Advance staff, so I was nearly giddy to find that another old friend from the Obama campaign, Reggie Hubbard, was coming in to handle Press Advance.

The remainder of the team, and the Sanders campaign's production capabilities, were also a happy surprise.

Due to the last-minute nature of Sanders' campaign scheduling and the campaign's large war chest, Levitt had wisely hired two professional production companies with a large amount of production equipment, large number of vehicles and staff, and a national network of other production companies. They could load their trucks with an array of equipment (we call it the "show in a box") and drive them overnight to venues anywhere in the country, find union labor to help, and arrive in time to build the site. (Presidential campaign event sites are really ad hoc television studios. Everything you might find in a studio has to be in place: lighting, audio, primary and secondary camera locations, direct feeds.)

I didn't learn of the campaign's production-on-the-fly capability until the Advance team, particularly my Site 1, Tyler, arrived. He knew the technical aspects of production and was already a seasoned professional at presidential-level Advance due to sheer repetition after only six weeks on the road. He had already been the victim of many one- and two-day Advance trips.

Given the late hour, rather than attempting any creative flights of fancy with a unique site, I chose a convention center, Bartle Hall, to hold the rally. Convention centers are sterile, unimaginative environments, but they are purpose-built. It gave me a giant open footprint to build the site and provided a lot of convenience for our production team and the Secret Service, including an enclosed arrival point for the motorcade and minimal security needs. I always want those guys and gals in Federal law enforcement—the hard-working men and women, but mostly men, of the Secret Service—to know I'm thinking of them too. Showing a little sensitivity for their concerns often comes in handy.

By Tuesday afternoon I was gaining confidence in our ability to produce a quality event. After a late-night and very early morning "build" and an 8 a.m. sweep by officers with dogs, we were ready at 10 a.m. on Wednesday, February 24— game day.

We designed the site to look good (as if it was packed full with supporters) on television with an audience of as few as twenty-five hundred people. At least two thousand people were already lined-up at the doors when they opened.

The First Bernie Moments

Sanders' charter jet landed at the Charles B. Wheeler Downtown Kansas City airport a few minutes earlier than scheduled, at 11:55 a.m. From the first moment of my interaction with him he appeared concerned, as I'd been warned was his constant state.

As he loitered outside of his OV (official vehicle) on the tarmac while waiting for the press and staff to unload and get into the motorcade, I walked over to introduce myself. I extended my hand, told him my name and that I was his Lead Advance for the trip. His response seemed to be one of alarm, as opposed to one of the more socially expected reactions, such as "Nice to meet you."

"So," he said gruffly, doing his best Larry David impersonation, "are you on staff?"

He wanted to know if he was paying me. To him, "advance" was an unnecessary expense.

"For all intents," I told him, "I'm your staff for this trip. But I'm volunteering."

That seemed to calm him. He nodded, but didn't say anything. I told him there was a large crowd to see him at the convention center and he said "good" and got into his car.

I have a photo of that interaction on the tarmac that was sent to me by the campaign's photographer. The expression on Bernie's face is, bless his heart, consistent with his public persona. He looks as if he just reached hour six of a twelve-hour enema. I look as if I'm being forced to watch it.

Sanders' expression never changed throughout the trip, even when grimacing through attempted smiles in front of the cameras. Nor did his gruff, off-handedly accusatory tone when he was talking with me or other members of the Advance team, always prefaced with the question, "So, are you the Advance guys?" even after the question had been asked and answered a few times already. It was true that he had no concept of what we do, or what we did to produce the day's media events and private meetings.

Knowing he doesn't like to be "handled" and with very few ways he could get lost, I remained as distant as possible. I counted on Tyler to answer any of his questions about the rally, and he and Reggie controlled most of the moving parts. A large crowd showed up, and while it took them more than four hours to pass through the mags, everyone got in by the time Bernie was half-way through his speech. While not a great situation, at least it wasn't a disastrous imposition on all of those who took the time out of their day to see Senator Sanders. The crowd seemed pleased.

The rally and the pre-rally press interviews and meetings with local organizers and an uncommitted super delegate happened as planned. It was a successful rally, a successful trip, and Bernie got back into the motorcade, cancelled a planned OTR (off-the-record, seemingly impromptu) stop at a local barbeque joint as we were departing Bartle Hall en-route (in other words, at the last second), went back to the airport and hung around there for almost an hour, then left.

One clear impression of the day stood out in my mind— the never-changing demeanor of Bernie and his body guy/primary interlocutor, Shannon. Humorless. They sent a message, and the message was, "This is grave business, and our next step may be off a cliff, so, somber-up." Pleasantness was frowned upon, literally. Every discussion, every brief interaction, carried the same burden of urgent solemnity. I have to admit that's not how I like my politics.

Both gentlemen were either taking themselves far too seriously or were keenly aware of their limitations and therefore scared down to their socks. After only one trip it was too soon for me to form an opinion; my interactions with them were too fleeting to judge whether their cemetery manner was indicative. But I've seen a hundred candidates and campaigns with that persona, and it seemed they were way beyond their depth in this endeavor. I just didn't know if they knew it.

The Second Advance Trip

It shouldn't have come as a surprise that Bernie needed to come back to Kansas for an event prior to its caucuses. Marc emailed me on Saturday, February 27, with the request, and once again I pulled a Frank Burns. Remembering my mortgage, I agreed to accept their day rate for this trip, which sadly takes some of the nobility out of the mission and makes me feel beholden to listen to people such as Bernie and Shannon.

The campaign wanted to hold a rally in either Lawrence or Topeka, on Thursday evening, March 3, which allowed four full days to do the Advance. Aces.

After another frantic Sunday venue search, on Monday I chose a 6,000-person capacity livestock arena in the Douglas County 4-H Fairgrounds in Lawrence, a five-minute drive from the University of Kansas— a natural audience for Bernie. I would have preferred a venue on campus. On the plus side, the acoustics in a venue with dirt floor are really good, and it was different from all of the other Sanders events being held all over the country. It screamed Kansas.

Once again, the Sanders Advance team, all new faces to me, were a happy surprise. Levitt had either chosen well or trained well or both.

The Sanders airplane arrived in Kansas over an hour early and I recommended, through Shannon, that Bernie do an OTR "town walk" in downtown Lawrence, where he'd be guaranteed to find a friendly crowd.

Stepping out of the motorcade, Bernie was concerned, again, about the situation. The nature of his questions as we walked to Massachusetts Street made it appear to me that he'd never set foot in Kansas. It might just as easily have been Mars. I was feeling confident in an environment with which I was familiar, so I didn't keep my distance from him in case he had any questions. He did.

"I thought we were in Kansas last week," he said.

"No sir, that was Kansas City, Missouri."

"So this is Kansas?"

"Yes sir, Lawrence, Kansas, forty miles west of Kansas City."

"What kind of reception will we get here?"

"They will love you here. Lawrence is a very blue island in a sea of red."

"Why?"

"The University of Kansas is here, and the town was settled by Eastern liberals prior to the Civil War. Despite the best efforts of pro-slavery guerillas at the time, and Republican gorillas now, it maintains the tradition. Around here we call the rest of Kansas 'Brownbackistan.'"

"Oh," he said. Apparently, he had heard that there's no smiling in politics.

With that, before we reached our starting point on Massachusetts Street, a family of four with a twelve-year old son wearing a Bernie Sanders t-shirt came walking toward us completely unaware that they were about see the man himself. It was the perfect start of an OTR, and a completely spontaneous occurrence. Imagine my surprise that a lovely family who happened to be friends of mine spontaneously left the Fairgrounds arena site after only one phone call from me alerting them to the OTR and offering them a personal introduction to the candidate. I love spontaneity.

It was a Hallmark moment. The media in tow with us lapped it up. The family got their photo with Bernie and Bernie was pleased to see his first locals "in the wild" so to speak, and they were supporters. (Later, when the family arrived back at the packed arena, I made sure that one of my Site Advance guys was there to escort them in to see his speech.)

Bernie walked and shook hands along several blocks of Massachusetts Street, where he was greeted enthusiastically. He even stopped at one point to go into a barber shop for a haircut.

One occurrence stood out in my mind. After Sanders spent several minutes getting a haircut, during which I remained outside and organized the gathering crowd, he exited the barber shop and paused to see which way to go. He looked around and finally looked at me. I assumed he was looking for his Advance person for direction, so I motioned to him, very subtly, to come my way. He clearly saw me motion, and clearly saw the group of people waiting patiently to shake hands with him. The moment he saw me attempt to draw him in my direction, on the sidewalk where he was already standing, he pivoted forty-five degrees and walked in the most inopportune direction, across the street, in front of traffic.

It was the oddest thing, like a child throwing a mini-tantrum to show who's boss. Since then, I've heard from other Sanders Advance staffers that they had experienced the same phenomenon. He didn't accept unsolicited suggestions of any kind, including the most basic ones regarding where to go next.

I didn't attempt to provide any further direction, logistical or otherwise. He could either follow my lead or not, and he obviously preferred being his own Lead.

Maybe it's just his manner, but he didn't appear comfortable meeting people in this unscripted environment. He didn't look them in the eye while he shook hands. As he walked, he held out his hands at his sides and kept moving, face forward, with only the briefest glances to spot the hands coming at him, making only furtive eye contact with a few.

The Douglas County Fairgrounds 4-H Livestock Arena

Once again, the mags were a bottleneck as the line of people stretched over a quarter-mile around the Fairgrounds. We placed loudspeakers outside to broadcast Sanders' speech to those who were still waiting when he began, but the sound only reached thirty yards.

Bernie was aware of the long line and was irritated, but it was unclear at whom. Backstage he spoke loudly at no one in particular, "This is unacceptable, gawddammit." When Service told him that the crowd was being moved into the arena as fast as possible, he said it again, "Gawddammit, this is unacceptable."

The one thing he could control, because it was his last event of the day, was the length of time he would wait to speak in order to allow more people into the building. It was made clear to me that *that* discussion was a non-starter. He would only wait an extra ten minutes. I could understand. It had been a long day and he was, after all, seventy-four years old.

He gave the same stump speech I'd heard in Kansas City.

The rally was fine. The entire crowd got into the arena by mid-speech, the visuals were rousing, the acoustics were great, Bernie grimaced as he shook hands along the "rope line" - a set of connected metal bike racks. Afterward he met briefly with an uncommitted super delegate from the area, then we spent forty-five minutes in the motorcade travelling the back roads of Kansas from Lawrence to the Topeka airport. Why we took the back roads rather than the interstate highway on the trip back was a mystery. I didn't bother to ask my Secret Service counterpart. He'd been through enough.

Bernie got on the plane and left, once again with no formalities or civilities. I supposed he was tired.

The Third, and Last, Advance(s)

Return with me now to the beginning of this story, on my third Advance, starting in Columbia, Missouri and ending in Springfield – the single strangest Advance trip of my entire career.

Another friend from 2008— I'll call her Susan— who had been appointed deputy director of Advance and taken over the slating of Advance teams, called me on March 9 to ask if I'd do one more trip.

Game day would be on March 12. When I balked, she played the "friend" card.

"I don't know what I'll do if you say no. I don't have anyone else," she told me.

After such a ringing endorsement, how could I resist.

Bernie had already done Missouri events in Kansas City (mine) and St. Louis, and they wanted a rally in anther town.

"How about Springfield?" I asked. "It's the third largest city in the state." It's also a town with which I'm very familiar.

"I'll ask Scheduling and get back to you," she promised. Within the hour she called back to tell me they decided to go to Columbia, Missouri. It sounded reasonable. With 35,000 students in town, we'd be guaranteed a huge crowd, if I could find a venue large enough.

The next morning, I was out early to pick-up a rental car and drive two hours to Columbia where, beginning at noon, I scoured the town for venues. There were none available, either on the campus of MU or off-campus. Not surprisingly, most venues in Columbia that are large enough to hold a rally are located on-campus, and those located off-campus are only a few minutes away because, well, it isn't New York.

Twelve hours and hundreds of phone calls, emails, texts, and site visits later, I found an obscure livestock arena in the agriculture area of MU's campus. They called it the "drone dome" because the School of Journalism was using it from time to time for students' drone piloting practice, a new discipline in the day's media universe. After peering in the windows at 1 a.m. I decided we would make it work for our rally. At 7:30 the next morning, Friday, I was knocking on doors in the Administration building and by 8:30 a.m. I had secured MU's approval.

With little more than a day remaining to produce and promote our rally, the Advance team kicked in to overdrive. Our first look inside the building was at 9 a.m.; we designed the event and sent our orders for site-specific production equipment by 10 a.m. and conducted meetings with everyone whose help we needed. Walk-throughs and logistics with Secret Service were completed by noon. An hour later I was told by Sanders headquarters that my Advance team and I should "stand down for the time being" because "there might be a problem." At 4 p.m. I was informed that we were moving the rally to Springfield. It was at that moment that I realized what "the problem" was.

Bernie had been told that he was going to Columbia the next day and remembered, or was told, that there had been recent racial unrest on campus. Next, he remembered the previous August in Seattle when Black Lives Matter activists stormed the stage where he was speaking, at which moment he decided he didn't want to take the chance of it happening again. So he instructed his Scheduling office to cancel the event and move it somewhere else. If they had bothered to ask me, I would have told them that the chance of disruption was miniscule. The Sanders campaign in Columbia, Missouri, had an on-going, mutually supportive relationship with the MU campus group One Nine Five Zero, which has a beef with MU's administration, *not* the Sanders campaign or any other presidential campaign. Hell, I would have invited the One Nine Five Zero leaders to meet with Bernie prior to the rally, then given them prime seats.

Staff Advance and Secret Service Advance teams de-camped Columbia, leaving behind dozens of confused Columbians with no more than a curt "we had a scheduling conflict," and headed for

Springfield, two and a half hours away, arriving at the JQH Arena on Missouri State University's campus at 7 p.m. The venue had been found and secured by Susan, who was simultaneously making cupcakes out of the cow pies that the campaign's senior leadership had dumped on her when they decided to add or move five other events on the schedule, including five other Advance teams, within a matter of the next two days.

The JQH Arena was a vastly different space than the drone dome at MU. It turned into a very long night with the arena staff, our contractors and our Secret Service counterparts.

With no time to order more equipment for an eight-thousand-person venue with no overflow space, we had no choice other than to use the staging, lighting, audio and security barricades for the three-thousand-person venue in Columbia (which had a lovely, contained overflow space where we could put additional loudspeakers).

In addition, the massive new venue required crowd logistics (the strategy and control necessary to move people into the right seats in the right order to ensure good visuals) that were highly complex. Ultimately, we had no idea how many Springfieldians would show up for a Bernie rally the next day after it had only been announced to the public at 9 p.m. that night. If only a couple thousand attended, they had better be sitting in the right places for the media shots.

I called Susan that night, late, after 11:30 p.m. her time when I knew she'd still be working, to voice my dissatisfaction. I asked her, "Do you mind if I vent about this, knowing that none of it is your fault? I know you must be going through your own kind of hell there at headquarters."

She was more than willing to hear my complaints, and did so in good, if not great, humor. She already knew what we were going through because she was tasked with inflicting it upon us, and she agreed it was political malpractice. In addition, she had a story of her own more horrendous than I could have possibly imagined, also inflicted upon her by the Sanders campaign.

"You know, I broke my knee on an Advance trip a few weeks ago, and they had to airlift me to a hospital because it was so bad," she said. "Well, since then, I've been in a cast up to my hip and the campaign has put me up in a hotel near headquarters so I can work out here slating teams and working as Marc's deputy. Well, today, in the midst of having to find teams for five new cities, scheduling five new venues and moving your team to Springfield, and having had no sleep in three days because this scheduling thing has been an on-going problem, the campaign told me I had to check out of my hotel room and go to an unfurnished apartment they rented for me. They told me that they'd ordered a bed to be delivered, but I had to build it myself."

My mood lightened considerably. Susan's story was so bad I could only laugh in disbelief. All in a moment my predicament seemed small. "That's beyond my ability to comprehend. No one's that heartless," I said.

"I'm not exaggerating," Susan said. "They sent a young woman from the campaign to tell me and give me the keys to the apartment. I just looked at her and said 'You have to be kidding. Look at me. I can't even bend over much less build furniture.'"

"So they've kicked you out of your hotel room and sent you to an unfurnished apartment? When did this happen?" I asked.

"Yesterday. The girl from the campaign felt so bad she went to the apartment and built the bed for me," Susan said. "In the meantime,

I'm still trying to find people I can slate for the Advance teams I'm sending out tomorrow for the next day's events."

"Your situation is so awful you've shamed me into a good mood," I said. "At least my agony will soon end; yours will continue for some time to come. I feel terrible for you, but thank you for sharing."

"Any time, Jacques."

We talked for another ten minutes as Susan described her impossible mission over the next two days, her current living conditions (Spartan at best), and her desire for an alcoholic beverage despite the fact that she doesn't drink. When we hung up my problems seemed inconsequential.

My team and I departed the JQH Arena at 1 a.m., I checked-in to the motel at 1:30, slept until 6 a.m. and we arrived back at the arena at 6:30 for the load-in.

From 6:30 until 4 p.m. it was a sprint for the Advance team and our production contractors to complete the thousands of details, and hundreds of tweaks, necessary to produce a seamless, high impact nationally televised presidential campaign event. The arena would have looked good on TV if only two thousand people attended, but we were prepared to accommodate up to eight thousand if needed, with appropriate lighting schemes to either hide empty space or highlight full seats.

If it was a small crowd, they had better be sitting in the right seats to look like a big crowd on television and in the newspapers . . . with the remainder of the arena darkened to the point of oblivion. If a big crowd happened, I wanted the TV cameras and still photographs to see it all.

Danny DeVito, No Danny DeVito

In the midst of the madness at mid-afternoon I received a call from a staffer in Sanders' Scheduling office asking if I'd be able to arrange for transportation and an escort for actor/producer/director Danny DeVito. He would arrive at the airport at 7:30 p.m. and wished to attend the rally.

Needless to say, this added a note of excitement we hadn't expected. I knew the Advance team would be thrilled to "host" Mr. DeVito at their rally, and it was easy enough to arrange. I called some friends, a reliable couple who live near Springfield and hadn't planned to attend the rally, and asked them to do the honors. They immediately set to work washing and cleaning their car in preparation.

A half hour later I received another call from the Scheduling office asking for more details on the rally, confirming my ability to transport Mr. DeVito and confirming his arrival at 7:30 p.m. via commercial airline.

At that point I told my Advance team that Mr. DeVito would be attending, which had the desired positive effect. The team was tired and this was a pleasant bonus for their labors.

Another half hour passed and Scheduling called one last time to confirm all the details of Mr. DeVito's travel and his place in the program. When she confirmed the airline and flight number it occurred to me (finally) that the Springfield-Branson National Airport doesn't have a ton of in-bound or out-bound flights in the evening hours, especially from major carriers, especially on weekends.

"I have a really absurd question," I said. "Is he flying into the Springfield, Missouri airport?"

"It says Kansas City airport in my notes," she answered.

"Is that Kansas City International?"

"I'll check," she said, then shuffled through a few papers. "It says Kansas City airport. Is that different from where you are?"

"It's in the same state," I said, "but if Mr. DeVito's plane arrives on time to the Kansas City airport and you immediately put him on a private jet and fly him to Springfield where the rally is, he'll get here in time to wave goodbye to Bernie as his motorcade departs the arena."

"It's that far?" she asked.

"If he drove from KCI to Springfield it would take over three hours. Flying takes an hour but it's a moot point. He wouldn't make it anyway and the campaign won't pay for a private jet."

"I'm sorry to have put you through all this," she said. "I'll let everyone know."

I called my friends who had agreed to do escort duty and called it off. They were gracious enough not to hold it against me.

It was an amusing aside in a day that was just getting started.

Doors Open, Sort Of

At 4 p.m.— the appointed time— the Secret Service opened the mags, all three of them, starting a veritable trickle of Bernie supporters into the arena. By the time our motorcade arrived at 6:30 p.m. only seven hundred fifty people were inside and the line outside wrapped around the entire arena, back up the street on the other side, across the street and up that block for another two hundred yards. It was easily a quarter-mile long.

My heart sank when I saw it. After almost forty years of fighting the battle of the mags with the Secret Service I knew there was nothing we could do. The only solution at that point is to wait as long as possible and ask the candidate, the "principal," to ask his Lead Agent to open up the mags and allow everyone who is still waiting to get in. The thinking is that the bad guys won't wait in line for three hours . . . they are usually close to the front. (When I mentioned that concept to my Service counterpart for the trip he said, "What about psychopaths?" "You convinced me," I replied.)

In the past this tactic was a reliable last resort. The "assassins like to be close to the front of the crowd" concept was told to me by a few Secret Service agents in the '70s through the 90s, and I had used the "request from the principal" as recently as the Obama campaign in '08, when I asked then-Senator Obama to ask his Lead agent to open the mags on a few occasions. However, given the increasingly nasty nature of the 2016 campaign and the violence that was just beginning to take on more ominous tones at Trump rallies, I was reluctant to suggest it. (Two days later when I called a couple of my Secret Service colleagues from the Springfield trip, I was informed that they wouldn't have opened the mags even if Senator Sanders requested it, which was news to me. I had no idea if this was a new Secret Service policy nationally or just within the Kansas City Field Office.)

Once Sanders was in the Holding Room, his body guy, Shannon, asked me to come in and explain the situation along with the Secret Service. First, I re-introduced myself and my role as his Lead Advance.

Senator Sanders was clearly bothered by the number of people still waiting in line, and I was in rare form due to lack of sleep or any concern about having a future with the Sanders campaign. As always, the Secret Service were stoic, professional, and straightforward—to a point. They didn't affix blame.

Free from trepidation about speaking the unvarnished truth, I was pleasantly blunt. "We always have too few mags," I told Sanders. "Service never brings enough under the best of circumstances." I smiled at the senior agents in the room. "But in this case the problem is completely self-inflicted. *We* did this. Yesterday morning, we had a venue in Columbia that held three thousand. After we moved here we had exactly twenty hours to set-up this venue, which holds eight thousand. Our campaign did this. This was our decision. Service doesn't have the ability to make more mags appear on a moment's notice."

Bernie didn't like hearing it. When I said, "Our campaign did this" I meant "He did this." It was *his* decision to cancel Columbia. He was clearly more agitated at the end of my explanation than at the beginning, and clearly didn't understand the process of pushing people through mags, which seemed odd to me. It's what you get when you accept Secret Service protection.

The Secret Service appeared content with my explanation, possibly even happy. When I suggested that we could shut down the mags at some point and let everyone in, the Lead Agent offered a comment about needing the mags so security isn't compromised. "Someone at the back of the line could come in with a weapon and hand it to a person who is closer to the front, and anywhere inside the arena is close enough to be within a reasonable security perimeter anyway."

Given the mood of the country, I was already halfway there when he made the comment.

Once his Secret Service agents left the Holding Room Sanders asked me, "Why aren't you out there moving people faster?"

As a curmudgeon-in-training myself, I was becoming agitated. "The only real solution is to tell Service to shut down the mags and let everyone in. That's the choke point and there is nothing other than that we can do about it. Now, shutting them down isn't something I feel comfortable with at this point, given what just happened last night at the Trump rally, but it's the only real solution."

Bernie complained a few more times that it was gawddammed unacceptable and made an attempt to give me an order. He started in a loud, clear, forceful manner, but his voice trailed-off at the end as if he was just hearing the idea for the first time when it came out of his mouth and he realized how meaningless it was. As he said it, he turned his head and walked away to the other side of the Hold. "Just . . . go out and get people in as fast as possible without com-promising . . . "

He didn't finish pronouncing the word "compromising" before not even speaking the word "security." It was late, he had to be tired, and I tried to tread softly and maintain a pleasant demeanor.

"We're doing our best, sir."

Once we were outside the Hold, Shannon turned to me and said "Thank you for your honesty."

After a half hour of short media interviews prior to the rally, Bernie was out of his Holding Room, walking the backstage hallway of the arena, stoop shouldered, irritated, looking for more explanations.

A few agents and I stood in a corner of the hallway with Bernie and explained the mag situation again, updated him on the crowd, and when the conversation turned to the Service's management of the mags, I pointed out once again that the Secret Service had twenty hours to do what they needed for this trip, and had to work with the equipment they'd had the day before, before *we* switched cities.

At some point I also mentioned off-handedly that there were four "protectees" in Missouri at that very moment. One, Ted Cruz, was less than three miles away at Evangel University. "Which means they've shipped mags into Missouri from all over the country just for tonight," I pointed out. "They're mag'd out. Ultimately this is about Congressional budget cuts. They don't have the budget to acquire more mags for election years."

The Lead Secret Service Agent for the trip looked at me and smiled. He liked that.

Bernie didn't. A couple of agents had told me that Bernie voted for recent cuts to the Secret Service's budget. Secret Service agents, being trained as investigators, are able to find out such things.

"Sir," the Lead Agent said to Senator Sanders, "all of those people are wearing coats, and there are a lot of handbags and backpacks. If they were wearing t-shirts and shorts it would go faster, and we have no control over that."

Unsatisfied, Bernie walked back to his Hold, but a few minutes later he was out roaming the hallways again. My Site 1, Drew, was updating me about the pre-program and the media when Bernie approached us. He raised his voice as he got up in our grills. "So, are you the Advance guys?" he barked. Since there was no way in the world he could not know the answer to that question, which he asked a lot, I assumed it was his way of saying "Howdy."

A diatribe followed. "Why are you standing heeah talking?" he continued without missing a beat. "Youah wasting time. Why aren't you out getting people in quicka? Youah standing heeah wastin' time, what's wrong with you?" he bellowed. "Youah not doing youah jobs. You should be out moving people quicka."

Drew was calm. "We have two hundred volunteers out there trying to move the line as quickly as possible." He'd been harassed by Bernie before.

"Well, theyah not doing a very good job," he said forcefully, just below a yell. "Youah wasting time. Why aren't you out there getting people in? Why aren't you finding people in t-shirts and shorts and getting them to the front of the line?" He was hectoring us. It was the only word for it. On top of it, he'd made one of the least helpful (to be diplomatic) suggestions I'd heard in, well, my entire Advance career.

I couldn't help but smile. I turned to my right and looked at Bernie and smiled. Big. The image of going out and pulling people from somewhere back in the line based on their attire and moving them up to the front, and the resulting riot that would occur, tickled me. The fact that it came out of the mouth of a man who claims to have good judgement, while he thinks that those about him have none, tickled me more.

Bernie was not amused. As it was explained to me later by the director of Advance, "He doesn't do mirth."

Undoubtedly Bernie took my reaction as an insult. "Stop talking and get the hell out of heah. Go get people in fastah. Go. Stop wasting time."

We walked away where Drew could brief me in private, and I asked him put our local Field organizers on stage for their "pitch" immediately, then he should personally introduce Congresswoman Tulsi Gabbard and former President and CEO of the NAACP Ben Jealous, who were on the trip with Bernie. I suggested that he should tell them all to talk as long as they liked, which was a first for me.

Assuming that Senator Sanders had gone back to Hold when we walked away, I was surprised to see him ten minutes later backstage, immediately behind the curtain, listening to the field organizers pitch. Congresswoman Gabbard and Ben Jealous were standing nearby waiting for their introduction. Sanders spotted me as I walked by nearly thirty feet away and he yelled, "Are you the Advance Lead on this trip?"

I walked to him and answered, "Yes, sir."

"Well, you didn't do a very good job," he bellowed, "a bad job."

Shocked by the public rebuke and happy to take the heat for my mistakes, I scanned my memory for screw-ups. Not finding any, my back stiffened. I looked him in the eye and replied unapologetically, "Sir, if you knew what we'd been through, you wouldn't say that."

So, he said it again, in front of everyone. "Well, you didn't do a very good job." He also was unapologetic.

My back stiffened further and my powers of diplomacy left the building. "If you knew what you were talking about, you wouldn't fucking say that."

It was as much of a surprise to me as it was to Bernie, the difference was that I was tickled the moment I heard it leave my lips. He deserved it, and I knew immediately that it was about to become one of the Advance war stories that we seasoned veterans love to tell.

Bernie was apoplectic. He could barely speak. After grumbling something incoherent he held out his arm and pointed his grizzled finger at me and grunted, "We'll talk."

I looked him straight in the eye. "I bet not," was my reply. I knew there would be no further conversation. I didn't know exactly what was going to happen, but I knew I'd never be speaking with the Bern again.

I walked back to the Staff Holding room and called Marc, who was already on the phone with someone about the incident, which had only occurred less than a minute before. Sanders and his inner circle seemed to relish feeling put-upon and they were in full serious crisis defense mode.

Marc's first words were: "First, let me say that I apologize, whatever happened. What the hell happened?"

I explained, and added my commentary, "You don't treat your staff like that," I said.

"You don't treat *anyone* like that," he said. Marc apologized again and added a few pointed comments of his own.

Within a few more moments Sanders' campaign manager, Jeff Weaver, who had kept his distance for the entire trip, made his dramatic entrance into the Staff Hold, with Shannon in tow.

He rushed toward me, practically frothing at the mouth. "Get the fuck out of here. Give me your fucking pin and get the fuck out of here." Shannon was stone faced and silent, as always, even when things were going well.

"Excuse me for a moment, Marc," I spoke into the phone, "Jeff just arrived." Then, speaking to Jeff and Shannon, "Are you guys going to be mean to me?" It was beyond my ability to stifle the smile, again.

Jeff was red-faced. "Just get the fuck out of here. Give me that fucking security pin." He looked as if he was about to yank it from my lapel himself, but refrained.

"Looks like I'm being kicked out of the rally," I told Marc. "I don't have transportation back to the airport arrival site to get my car."

"I'll send a cab for you," Marc said, and apologized again.

As any good Advance Lead should, I had several extra security pins in my pocket "just in case." Five in fact. It occurred to me that it would significantly enhance the story if I walked out, put another one on my lapel, and walked back in, only to have it yanked from my lapel again, and did that five times. I pictured me playing Harpo in what would have been a scene from a Marx Brothers movie, and figured the Secret Service agents guarding the doors wouldn't care. I wasn't a threat, and they liked me better than they like Bernie anyway. I opted not to go to the trouble, seeing myself as more of a Groucho type when these situations occur.

Once outside, Susan called to inquire. She also apologized, and added her own pointed commentary.

Their support was appreciated. Despite my amused reaction, and fact that I felt justified responding to Bernie's repeated rude behavior, I've never told a major presidential candidate that he didn't know what the fuck he was talking about. It was good to know that Susan and Marc had my back, rhetorically. If I'd cared about continuing my role as a Sanders Advance person, that might have been a tougher task, but since that was not the case . . .

Postscript

The rally looked great on television that night and the next morning. At breakfast I saw my Site II, who told me that Bernie hated the lighting scheme, which kept darkened those parts of the arena not filled with people, and he demanded that all of the lights be turned on immediately. Happily, the lower levels of the arena eventually filled with enthusiastic bodies.

In the days that followed I talked with a few friends who were doing Sanders Advance. While my verbal interaction with Bernie was unique, the circumstances surrounding it were not.

The next day as I drove back to Kansas City, I called Marc to apologize to him, a courtesy that had eluded me in my disquieted state the night before. "Did I get you at a bad time?" I asked.

"No, I'm in the middle of building a site and I just sat down with a beer," he told me.

Both of these bits of information were quite surprising. The fact that the director of Advance was in the field building a site, and drinking a beer while he was doing it, said something, but I wasn't sure what.

"I hope last night doesn't cause problems for you," I told him.

"Not at all," he said. "They don't fire me, I fire them."

OK, I thought. That says everything. He was even less in the mood to be critiqued by Senator Sanders than I had been.

Ultimately it was an Advance trip of firsts for me. For the first time since beginning my Advance career in 1976, and in the ensuing thousands of presidential campaign Advance trips I've done since, (1) I was sent to city in which no venue would be approved because the entire city couldn't be approved in the candidate's mind, and (2) I was kicked-out of my own rally.

My experience was just the tip of the iceberg in terms of the demands placed on Sanders' Advance staff, and by extension on the Secret Service agents who are responsible for ensuring his safety, keeping in mind that they are people too, with families and regular Secret Service Field office responsibilities. Most young Staff Advance people don't have those constraints.

Such frenetic scheduling was normal for the Sanders campaign, and because both Staff and Secret Service kept pulling rabbits out of their hats, senior campaign leadership witnessed no reason to do things any differently.

Also unseen by Sanders was the impact that he had on the campaign's Field organization, which was left at a serious disadvantage when organizing their voter/volunteer/donor I.D. efforts to take advantage of their large crowds. I had to assume that this undermined the campaign, given the number of times it occurred nationally.

When Bernie announced his candidacy, I thought that like Don Quixote, Senator Sanders appointed himself knight errant, "to sally forth and right the world's wrongs." Unlike Sanders, the Lord of La Mancha's "eyes burned with the fire of inner vision."

Bernie's eyes burned with irritation.

It may or may not be important to remember that when Bernie decided to seek elective office, where he could fight the pantheon of wrongs vexing society—income inequality, economic opportunity, access to health care, racism, sexism and other evils—he chose Vermont. Being from Brooklyn, he might have tried to bloom where he was planted, but Vermont probably seemed the right place to exorcise society's demons.

Ultimately, he seems to have had an impact on the Democrat Party's policies, hopefully a good one. But as the Party found for the second time in the first two decades of this century, Vermont is not New York. If you can do it there, it doesn't necessarily mean you can do it anywhere.

EPILOGUE

How can you not love doing presidential-level advance. Every trip is an expedition into the unknown, an adventure with a mission. It is the ultimate all-access pass.

For a young man who was enthralled with national politics from childhood, as I was, it was the fulfillment of a dream, which is why I've remained involved for almost fifty years.

How did politics spark the interest of an otherwise dimwitted kid? It was television. The time was the late '50's and early '60's, when TV was becoming the dominant media. There were three networks and anyone you saw on TV was a celebrity, from presidential candidates to the local after-school kid's show host.

Either Huntley & Brinkley or Douglas Edwards or Walter Cronkite were always on before dinner, and all the national and international news could be reported in the span of a fifteen-minute newscast. The Kennedy campaign in 1960 were masters of the medium and they made it look glamorous. When Kennedy spoke, he cloaked public service in the vestments of honor and nobility.

By the time I started working on political campaigns television was firmly entrenched as the gold standard for communicating political messages. As an advance man working for Jimmy Carter in 1976, my job was all about that thirty to forty-five seconds of network news coverage that we could garner on the national evening news. If the cameras didn't get the shot, whatever "it" was never happened.

The time of day also mattered. The "news window" for doing a presidential campaign event meant that wherever in the U.S. it was taking place – a rally, a town hall meeting, a policy speech, etc. – it had to be completed in time for the news crews' video tape to be couriered to a television station that had the facilities to edit and uplink to a satellite. The deadline was 6:30 p.m. Eastern, in time for the evening news. Often that video had to be taken by motorcycle to the local airport and flown to a major-market TV station. By today's standards it was a cumbersome process.

As a result, the "event of the day" was usually scheduled no later than early afternoon, and it was a sign of trust to be assigned to the advance team tasked with creating that event. That legacy continues today; there will still usually be one event that a campaign will structure to be the biggest that day, but the nearly perpetual news cycle, the ability to edit, upload and broadcast video instantaneously, live coverage and the proliferation of media outlets, have diminished the concept of media deadlines.

By the end of the Carter administration cable news had just begun, marking a new era of coverage.

Interestingly, many of the lessons I learned in my first presidential campaign and during the Carter administration became touchstones for every advance I've done through twelve presidential campaigns and three administrations.

My very first advance trip for Jimmy Carter to Bismarck, North Dakota, in August 1976 was a revelation. Despite the training I'd received a few weeks earlier at the advance seminar in Atlanta, it blew me away that two guys, one of whom was a relative novice, had that much responsibility to create and produce the Democratic nominee's national media event…to create what everyone would see on television, and for that one moment define the candidate's image.

I was the second on the two-man team. The lead advance, Jim MacKinnon, at 27 years of age was one of the old guys as far as I was concerned. We were sent to do an event, the specific nature of which was left up to Jim.

Local political and civic leaders in Bismarck did have specific plans for Carter's visit, none of which were realistic given the schedule. Jim decided there was only time for an airport rally and diplomatically negotiated a happy acceptance from the townspeople.

The lead advance made all the critical decisions. He decided who would share the stage with Carter and who would be on the program, he brought-in marching bands from the local schools (to build the size of the crowd) and got them to coordinate a play list, got senior citizen centers to bus-in seniors, (for whom he provided seating, which also made the crowd look larger), he found all the resources for audio-visual production and site-building, including a flatbed trailer from a local farm to use as our stage, and importantly, he decided on the "visual" -- that all-important backdrop to Carter's speech.

MacKinnon made the decision to order an "environmental graphic" of a wheat scene because the price of wheat and support for agriculture were important issues for Carter. The scene was actually printed on wallpaper, which he bought from a company in Minneapolis. We glued and taped it to a 16-foot by 8-foot polyurethane backing, then stapled it to long 2x4's which we secured to the airport fence behind the lectern. We *thought* it was secured to the fence.

*Courtesy of the Elwyn B. Robinson Department of Special
Collections, Chester Fritz Library, University of North Dakota
Jimmy Carter in Bismarck, ND, 1976*

While I have no doubt that Jim was informing Carter headquarters of his decisions, they were his to make because they trusted him. He and I acted on those decisions without hesitation because there wasn't time to dither.

In addition to the evocative visual, stage guests, program and crowd building, Jim showed me how to think beyond the creativity of the "set-shot" to give an event soul and depth, and possibly create a memorable image.

When we picked-up the flatbed trailer that we were to use as our stage, I found an old horseshoe on the ground and picked it up, as I am wont to do. When we returned to headquarters in town, Jim decided to use it in our event. He would get a couple of cute children, (it's usually easy to find cute kids), and have them present it to Carter when he arrived on Peanut One. Jim took it outside and scraped it on the sidewalk to shine it up, and tapped in hard on the pavement to shake loose the manure still stuck it its nail holes. Most of it came out.

We got a green ribbon and tied it in bow, and on event-day the kids made their presentation on cue. The local press loved it. So did Carter. He took the horseshoe and hung it from a strap in the middle of a double seat across from his seat on Peanut One, and it remained there for the rest of the campaign, with the bow and a little manure in the nail holes.

The entire trip - event production, Jim's political adroitness and diplomacy and ability to control everything with quiet good humor – was a masterclass. I was lucky to have him as my first lead, and he served as a model when I started doing leads a year and a half later after joining Vice President Mondale's staff.

During that first year and a half of advance I learned that good leads were adept at creating an entire environment, using the resources at their disposal to enhance the visual components of our events, whatever type of events we were producing. The mediocre leads couldn't see beyond the lectern. The bad leads were assholes in addition to being mediocre.

Visually and emotionally, it would be the difference between watching a movie made by Steven Spielberg and one by Ed Wood.

Unexpectedly, I learned three more valuable lessons during that first trip for Carter when I thought there was nothing more to learn. The first was: "Don't stand in the press chute when the national press corps is running from their airplane to the press area." I was knocked on my butt by the CBS camera crew, when cameras were much larger and heavier than they are today. More than my ego was bruised.

The second lesson I learned is that jets create a lot of wind then they power-up to leave, also known as jetwash, and, stay with me here, a 16 x 8-foot sheet of polyurethane becomes a sail when it is hit with jetwash. I learned this lesson after our rally was over and Carter had gone back to Peanut One. As I was breathing a sigh of relief, nonchalantly watching the airplane turn and leave, I noticed a couple of Secret Service agents to my left who were looking to my right and laughing.

When I looked to my right, I saw our backdrop had been blown off the fence, 2x4's and all, and landed squarely on our senior citizens seating area. There were old people crawling around under the plastic amongst a jumble of chairs, trying to extricate themselves. It wouldn't have been funny except most of them were laughing. Two women had cuts on their heads. (I found out later they asked the campaign to pay $80 for their stitches. They said they didn't mind being wacked on head because they said they had such a good time.)

The third lesson I learned was really a reinforcement of what I'd been taught in advance school: "If the cameras didn't get it, it never happened." In this case we got lucky; when the backdrop attacked our senior citizens, the cameras were either turned-off or pointed in the wrong direction.

That would never happen today. The cameras are always rolling.

In the spirit of lightheartedness, leaving the weightier aspect of advance for another book, I'll share a few of the experiences, moments, challenges and people that stand out from this most interesting avocation over the course of forty-eight years:

Happiest surprise on a campaign advance trip: August, 2000, Gore presidential campaign…rolling into tiny Bellevue, Iowa at nearly midnight on a Saturday night to find a dismal little town and a scary-looking motel off a gravel road where my team and I were booked to stay. The campaign had asked me to advance a stop along Al and Tipper Gore's post-Democratic Convention roll-out, which was a river boat tour down the Mississippi. Bellevue was the site of a lock and dam, requiring the boat to pause there, and my team was tasked with producing a riverside rally. It felt dreary and depressing beyond words.

Then the unexpected occurred. I found the only other possible accommodations in town, the stunningly beautiful and not inexpensive Mont Rest Bed and Breakfast. The owner was a Democrat who agreed to match the cheap motel's rate for the entire team. We enjoyed gourmet breakfasts, and held our team meetings on the veranda with a stunning view overlooking the Mississippi. The owner,

Christine, connected us with every Democrat in the area. Bellevue turned out to be a lovely riverside town with a main street that offered perfect Midwest small town images; the rally was well-attended, colorful and enthusiastic. Al and Tipper had a good time, and the campaign chose video from that event to use in the first TV ad of the general election. Forgive the hyperbole, but it was magical.

Best departure from town after a trip: Obama's trip to Paris, 2008. I gave the Frenchman at the airport ticket counter my last Obama '08 button as a thank you for assigning me the exit row seat I wanted for the flight back to D.C. He was grateful, and gave me a pass to the first-class lounge. Having arrived at the airport hours early, I felt like I'd scored. Two hours later, after I took my seat on the airplane for departure, the same ticket agent got on the plane and asked me to follow him. He took me to a First Class seat and that's where I stayed, for the price of a campaign button. I believe the French liked Obama.

Best campaign: Obama, 2007 to 2009, Announcement Day to Inaugural Day. The Obama campaign's nascent Scheduling and Advance operation included people with whom I worked for John Kerry in 2004, and they asked me to advance the second event of his presidential campaign, February 11, 2007. It was a town hall meeting in Cedar Rapids, Iowa. That was the day I met Michelle and Barack and their family. (Everyone but Barack was already tired after the big announcement event in Illinois.)

At a time in a presidential campaign, almost a year before the Iowa caucuses, when most other candidates would be happy to attract fifteen voters in someone's living room, I booked a gymnasium that could hold 2,500 people, and the place was packed to capacity and beyond.

After about 75 advance trips (I lost track) as Obama's senior national lead advance through to the end of the campaign, I had the honor of coordinating day-one of the three-day Inaugural activities – the Inaugural Whistle Stop Tour from Philadelphia, through Wilmington, Delaware (where we picked-up the Bidens), then Baltimore and Washington, DC. It was January 17, which was also Michelle's birthday, so her staff decorated one of the train cars and we had a party. Malia and Sasha handed out cake to the revelers, and we all wore Hawaiian leis.

© Ron Soliman – USA TODAY NETWORK via Imagn Images
The 2009 Inaugural Whistle Stop

The Obama campaign was like the candidate - no drama. It was fun and we were full of hope. Such was also the case and my situation with the Kerry campaign in '04, but we lost, so…. heartbreak.

Strangest noise I ever heard come out of anyone's mouth, during a campaign or ever: It was a plaintive wail, or a high-pitched moan of agony – "Nooooooooooooooooooo." It went on for several seconds. It came from the mouth of our Rock Hill, South Carolina field coordinator when I told him that Obama had to cancel the next day's rally (because of his Senate schedule) that we had been working on for three days. The field coordinator had invited his parents from out of state, bought a new suit and gotten a haircut. I didn't feel too badly because the guy had not been very helpful to the advance team; he seemed more concerned with getting his picture taken with Obama and getting a security pin so he could clutch the candidate.

I told him we'd come back in a couple weeks and we did. He got his photo. I didn't give him a security pin.

Greatest cultural shock: Gore-Chernomyrdin Commission meetings, Moscow, December 1994…like walking back in time to the 1950's, as if we were in a black & white movie. It may not be the Soviet Union any longer, but the people haven't changed. No one will take responsibility or make a decision, no one will give a straight answer; they can't function without a person in a higher position of authority telling them what to do. Every time we visited a site, there were different contact persons with different non-committal views of the occasion.

I decided that we, the White House advance team, would take over all operations in the key site – The President Hotel, where all meetings and functions were held - once the Vice President arrived. We did, and the Russians didn't seem mind in the least. Someone was taking charge. I asked the U.S. Embassy to create credentials for the entire advance team written in Cyrillic (Russian) that stated we were with Vice President Gore's staff and were working with the Kremlin. We took control of the logistics of ceremonies, meetings and signings. We controlled Prime Minister Chernomyrdin's movements because he wouldn't leave Gore's side; he moved with us. On one occasion when I decided to completely re-stage a room for a press conference, I told the V.P. what we were up to and asked that he wait in a holding room with the P.M. while we reconfigured.

My Russian counterpart during the advance, a deputy minister, had two favorite expressions when I inquired about things we wished to do, and he used them both often without a hint of sarcasm or contradiction. The first was "Anything is possible." (Imagine it with a Russian accent.) The second was "It's impossible."

The Moscow airport was the worst aggressive mob scene I've witnessed. Russians seemingly have no concept of organization or forming lines of any kind. The Embassy staff that had been so attentive and courteous when our team arrived in Moscow, escorting us through the myriad Russian credential checks and bureaucratic niceties to facilitate our entry, changed after the V.P. departed and it was time for us to do so too. We were essentially dumped at the airport curb and told "Good luck." It was a nightmare. Maybe there was nothing our Embassy minders could do to alleviate that.

Despite the frustrations and nearly constant challenges, even that advance trip provided some memorable fun for the team. At the beginning of the trip, as I was sifting through the labyrinth of my U.S. and Russian contacts, I had no assignments, no tasks on which my team could begin working. With nothing for them to do, I told them to take the day off and explore. That night all ten of them went to the Moscow Circus, where one member of the team, a young innocent-looking blond chap from California, ended up being called to the stage to participate in the show at length, twice, to be part of the clown act. The team returned to our hotel brimming with stories about the evening.

White House Advance Team, Vanukova II Airport, Moscow, December 1994

Most reliably memorable and fun sight: A joint motorcade at night. The lead advance person sits in the Lead Marked Car of the motorcade along with his Secret Service counterparts. All the other vehicles are behind, and they string out for a distance, including two limos, staff vans, press busses, VIP guest vans, EMT, police and highway patrol. Often there are motorcycle cops zipping by to control intersections.

Presidential motorcades are long, vice presidential motorcades slightly less so, but when you do joint presidential/vice presidential trip and you have a joint motorcade, there can be 45 vehicles.

Do it at night with everyone's headlights on and lights flashing on all the cop cars, it is a little awe-inspiring. When viewed from the Lead Car, or from the last car in the motorcade, traveling around a long curve on the highway, it can be seen all at once, almost as a single being. Even the Secret Service agents sitting in the Lead Car with me enjoy the view.

It's the little things.

Most difficult trip: February 2008, New Orleans, Obama — tasked with producing a policy speech a day and a half after Mardis Gras ended. The team arrived during Mardis Gras and we were booked at a hotel in the French Quarter. It took hours to drive the last mile to get there. It was impossible to get anyone's attention much less find a site, secure contractors, publicize the event to draw a crowd, or do walk-throughs with staff and Secret Service. There wasn't a Democrat, civic leader, activist or academician to be found.

Unsurprisingly, most people, including all the local audio-visual contractors who are involved in Mardis Gras, also like to take off the day after it's over. No one cares that you've got the next President of the United States coming to town. It was as if we were in an empty ghost town that was packed with people.

After two days I was finally able to track down an intermediary, an out-of-town person, who was able to put me in touch with the president of Tulane University, which seemed like my best hope. I arranged to meet him in his office the next morning, the day after Mardi Gras ended.

As my team and I drove to meet him, the detritus of licentiousness was still evident everywhere, including floats on the side of the road with people passed-out on them in various poses. We had to back up the car so one of the people on my team could take a picture of an unconscious guy on whom someone had used a sharpie to paint huge eyebrows, a mustache and goatee. It looked like the guy was still breathing.

About 24-hours later Obama arrived, he did his policy speech in an auditorium at Tulane, it looked great, he had a responsive crowd, we did an OTR, (off the record movement), to one of New Orleans' fine local restaurants and the food was fantastic.

And I was forced to go to Mardis Gras, which I never, repeat never, would have done on my own. It was good to see it once, but not under those circumstances. It isn't easy to have fun when you're worried that you won't have anything for your principal to do when he arrives in town.

Best part of doing advance: The people. I have not said enough about the hundreds of people on hundreds of teams I've worked with through the years. Advance people are special. They have a spirit of camaraderie and dedication that is unique. They are all striving to catch lightning in a bottle on every trip. We develop a bond that is as strong as any between humans short of a foxhole. When the challenges seem insurmountable, advance staffers rise to the occasion every time. At least the people I worked with did.

In the high-stakes atmosphere of national politics, which is often rife with power plays and internal bickering, advance teams invariably work together and support one another in ways that are inspirational.

When the time comes, after a trip is completed, when I can introduce my teams to their "principals," (candidates, presidents, vice presidents, etc.), so they can be thanked, I have a habit of introducing them as "Your band of immortals," which is a compliment, but one tinged with irony. It's a perfect compliment because advance teams perform in heroic ways, and most often deserve the accolade, especially when the advance trip, in its entirety, has been particularly hard. Also, the term sounds grand.

As an old political operative, however, I understand that we, advance staffers, are not only replaceable but regularly replaced. As a person with an academic background in Iranian/Persian history, I connect us to the name "immortals" because it was given to an elite unit of the ancient Persian army and stemmed from the fact that every soldier who was killed or injured was immediately replaced with another that looked exactly like him. So, it appeared as if the army never died. Sometimes they would wear cloth over their faces to enhance the impact.

Advance teams share some of those characteristics.

In 1979, when I advanced Vice President Mondale's trip to Kansas City for a set of events supporting the mayoral candidacy of Bruce Watkins, I had a chance to work at length with a local barbecue restaurant owner who was a personal friend of the candidate. Our assistant in the V.P.'s advance office told me to watch out for him because he sounded mean over the phone.

He sounded mean in person too, but he was a good guy and good to work with. So much so that I invited him to the airport, along with the candidate, to meet Air Force Two. As we waited on the tarmac, he turned to me and asked, "Where do they find you guys? You all look the same, wear the same clothes, act the same. Do they get you guys off an assembly line? Where do they find you?"

I thought I knew what he meant. I looked like a generic a young white guy in a dark suit, the type you might expect to see working for the White House in the 1970's.

My response: "I promise you; they didn't find me. I found them."

It is still the case that most of us had to work hard get to do advance, but we've never been generic. We only looked that way. It takes many kinds of people with many kinds of skills to do advance.

I will end with a salute to the advance people with whom I've had the privilege and pleasure to work during these exiting, historic times. The vast majority believe, as do I, that working in politics is a noble mission. Most are brilliant, hard-working professionals who have the exceptionally special talent of making really big things happen in impossibly short periods of time under extremely stressful circumstances…and leaving behind nothing but positive memories… and positive media coverage.